WHY WAR?

WHY WAR?

IDEOLOGY, THEORY, AND HISTORY

Keith L. Nelson and Spencer C. Olin, Jr.

UNIVERSITY OF CALIFORNIA PRESS

Berkeley • Los Angeles • London

To Our Wives,
Paddy and Patty

University of California Press
Berkeley and Los Angeles, California

University of California Press, Ltd.
London, England

First Paperback Printing 1980
ISBN: 0-520-04279-4
Library of Congress Catalog Card Number: 78-51746
Printed in the United States of America

4 5 6 7 8 9

The paper used in this publication meets the minimum
requirements of American National Standard for
Information Sciences—Permanence of Paper for
Printed Library Materials, ANSI Z39.48–1984. ∞

Contents

Introduction

Potentially, history is an enormously rich resource for people
who govern. If the instances portrayed [here] are at all indica-
tive, such people usually draw upon this resource haphazardly
or thoughtlessly. By and large, those of us professionally occupied in teaching and writing history have put out little effort
to help them.

Ernest R. May, *"Lessons" of the Past* (1973)

Nothing is more urgent for historians than for them to analyze
their practice of generalization, to define the principal kinds of
generalization which they engage in, to subject these to critical
study, and to seek an organized, conscious view of elements
which have remained unorganized and unrecognized though
ubiquitous in historical writing.

David M. Potter, "Explicit Data and Implicit
Assumptions in Historical Study" (1963)

Though in general we agree with Harvard historian Ernest
May's recent assertion that, with help from professional
historians, foreign policy decision-makers can learn to "use"
history much more effectively,[1] we also believe it is pre-
sumptuous for historians to claim that their discipline can be
useful without first paying more attention to generalization
and to the roots of generalization in theory. Unfortunately,
the historical profession still makes a fetish of complexity,
and most historians eschew broad hypotheses and categoriz-
ing systems. They tend to emphasize the *uniqueness* of situations (taking a descriptive, idiographic approach) rather
than the *similar and recurrent elements* of diverse experiences (which requires a generalizing, nomothetic approach).
This "historicist" stress on complexity and on the unique

1. Ernest R. May, *"Lessons" of the Past: The Use and Misuse of
History in American Foreign Policy* (New York: Oxford University
Press, 1973), pp. ix-xiv.

aspects of events has diminished the meaning of history by robbing it of much of its power for comprehending the world in which we live.

One of the most pertinent illustrations of this general tendency is the manner in which historians have studied the causes of war. Of all the problems confronting foreign policy decision-makers, the problem of war is surely the most critical. Furthermore, there would seem to be enormous potential for significant historical comparisons and projections about war. Yet historians characteristically describe and analyze each war as a thing unto itself. They have ignored the possibility that the occurrence *and* the process of war follow discernible historical patterns to a much greater extent than is commonly recognized.

We contend that historians can and should examine the recurrent elements in international conflict with the aim of making the study of the past more relevant to everyone, policy-makers and citizens alike. Nonetheless, before we can begin to develop the kind of comparative, synoptic, and integrated approach to war that is required if the history of the subject is to be truly "useful," it is necessary to examine carefully the role of theory in scholarly writing about war. This is because only through the use of theory can a statement of any *general* applicability be made or tested. It is also because the notion of theory itself has often been misunderstood and badly defined. We would distinguish, for example, between "theory," on the one hand, and a "historical explanation" of a single event (such as the assassination of John F. Kennedy), on the other, since a theory must be able to account for two or more comparable events.

What, then, is a theory and how does it work in historical analysis? A theory is by definition an abstract, conjectural representation of reality. By organizing a picture of the real world, a theory assigns significance to certain facts and speculates about existing and changing relationships between them. It thus serves as a guide to empirical research on historical problems, instructing us as to which questions

what is theory?

to ask of the data. It also serves to show us which of the occurrences of history may possibly be grouped into structural families. In sum, then, to theorize about war (or any apparently recurrent phenomenon) is to develop a set of general and interrelated statements about it that (1) are internally consistent, (2) permit us to explain or predict specific events, and (3) are thereby open to empirical testing.[2]

In a sense, of course, all historians, even those of historicist persuasion, rely on theory. Otherwise, they would simply be overwhelmed by the mass of information that confronts them. The fact remains, however, that few historians are explicit in their selection of theory or systematic in its application.

Nor are many historians or even theorists aware of

2. See Oran R. Young, "The Perils of Odysseus: On Constructing Theories of International Relations," in Raymond Tanter and Richard Ullman (eds.), *Theory and Policy in International Relations* (Princeton: Princeton University Press, 1972), p. 180; and Kenneth N. Waltz, "Theory of International Relations," in Fred I. Greenstein and Nelson W. Polsby (eds.), *International Politics* (Reading, Mass.: Addison-Wesley, 1975), pp. 1-85. On the importance of theory in the study of history see, among others, Othmar F. Anderle, "A Plea for Theoretical History," *History and Theory*, 4 (1964), pp. 27-56; Gareth Stedman Jones, "History: The Poverty of Empiricism," in Robin Blackburn (ed.), *Ideology in Social Science: Readings in Critical Social Theory* (New York: Pantheon, 1972), pp. 113-114; and Hayden White, "The Historian at the Bridge of Sighs," *Reviews in European History*, 1 (March 1975), pp. 437-445. As White asserts (p. 439): "[W]here there is no theory, there can never be anything resembling *usable* knowledge. And whether usable or not, where there is no theory, there can never be anything pretending to the status of scientific knowledge. Without theory, there is no way of directing experiments or even observations in cognitively responsible ways, no way of linking up one datum with another, or extrapolating from observed trends for purposes of predicting or forecasting, or of mediating between theory and practice on the one side or between contending theories on the other. Where there is no theory, not only is there no science, there is no possibility of objectivity at all." For a helpful discussion of the varieties of historical explanation as well as the role of assumptions and theory in history, see the essays by Louis Gottschalk, William O. Aydelotte, and David M. Potter in Louis Gottschalk (ed.), *Generalization in the Writing of History* (Chicago: University of Chicago Press, 1963), pp. 113-129, 145-194.

perhaps the most crucial fact about theory: namely, the close relationship between theory and "ideology." As human creations, theories derive from and reflect their creators' ideologies; that is, they are conditioned by the assumptions, beliefs, and ideas with which their creators envisage the world, both as it is and as it should be.[3] "Analytic work begins with material provided by our vision of things," the late economist Joseph Schumpeter once stated, "and this vision is ideologic almost by definition."[4] Considerations of

3. Alvin Gouldner, in his important work, *The Coming Crisis of Western Sociology* (New York: Avon Books, 1970), calls these metaphysical beliefs "domain assumptions." Gouldner posits two analytical aspects of theory formulation: (1) the superstructure of the theory (in which the explicitly formulated assumptions, concepts, and hypotheses are advanced), and (2) the infrastructure of the theory (which contains unstated and implicit assumptions, values, and beliefs). This infrastructure serves as a "silent partner" in the construction of the total theory. On this matter we have profited from an unpublished paper by Frederick R. Lynch, "Social Theory and the Progressive Era: Two Case Studies in the Sociology of Knowledge" (Pitzer College, Claremont, Calif., 1973).

4. Joseph Schumpeter, *History of Economic Analysis* (New York: Oxford University Press, 1954), p. 42. We hope it will be clear from our definition of the word "ideology" that we are using the term in a non-pejorative sense, i.e., to connote "sets of ideas by which men posit, explain and justify ends and means of organized social action, and specifically political action. . . ." rather than associating the term with falseness, deception, and distortion. See Martin Seliger, *Ideology and Politics* (New York: Free Press, 1976), p. 14. For a detailed examination of ideology, see Edward A. Shils, *The Intellectuals and the Powers and Other Essays* (Chicago and London: University of Chicago Press, 1972), pp. 23-41. An ideology differs from a "prevailing outlook" and its creeds, according to Shils (p. 24), "through its *greater explicitness*, its greater *internal integration* or *systematization*, the *comprehensiveness* of its scope, the *urgency* of its application, and the much higher *intensity of concentration* on certain central propositions or evaluations." (Emphasis in text.) Shils also points out (p. 26) that "ideologies insist on the primary value of the realization of principles in conduct." An ideology must advance a program designed to achieve certain ideals in practice. See also Clifford Geertz, "Ideology as a Cultural System," in David E. Apter (ed.), *Ideology and Discontent* (New York: Free Press, 1964); George Lichtheim, *The Concept of Ideology and Other Essays* (New York: Vintage, 1967); and Maurice Dobb, *Theories of Value and Distribution Since Adam Smith: Ideology and Economic Theory* (Cambridge: Cambridge University Press, 1973).

ideology are clearly *not* extrinsic to theory or therefore history, and we are dismayed by the degree to which this fact is overlooked or minimized by most formulators of theory and historians.[5]

This is not to say that we consider a theory necessarily valid or invalid because of its peculiar origins. There are too many historical instances of good ideas being found in "trash bins" for us to reach such a conclusion. Nor is it to say that we believe all theories to be equally successful or unsuccessful. On the contrary, we wish to suggest that, by increasing our consciousness of the subjective factors that influence theory building, we shall improve our ability to identify the implicit structures of theories, to test theories for validity, and in general to ascertain their usefulness.

In any case, our emphasis on the importance of ideology in the construction of theory should not be construed as an argument for ideology as the determining factor in history. In truth, we believe that ideologies are themselves largely the creation of historical forces and reflect the material interests, ideal aspirations, and psychological needs of the individuals, groups, and classes that assert them. Yet we are also convinced that approaching the problem of theory from the perspective of ideology enables us to discern "clusters" of theories about the causes of war and to reveal how each of those theories is rooted in fundamental assumptions about human beings and society. Not only is this of interest in itself, but it also affords a convenient means of showing

5. See, for example, Robert Dubin, *Theory Building* (New York: Free Press, 1969); Hubert M. Blalock, Jr., *Theory Construction: From Verbal to Mathematical Formulations* (Englewood Cliffs, N.J.: Prentice-Hall, 1969); Nicholas D. Mullins, *The Art of Theory: Construction and Use* (New York: Harper and Row, 1971); Paul Davidson Reynolds, *A Primer in Theory Construction* (Indianapolis, Ind.: Bobbs-Merrill, 1971); and Charles A. Lave and James G. March, *An Introduction to Models in the Social Sciences* (New York: Harper and Row, 1975). More sophisticated in this regard are Kenneth N. Waltz, *Man, the State, and War* (New York: Columbia University Press, 1959); and Kjell Goldmann, *International Norms and War Between States* (Stockholm: Läromedelfölagen, 1971).

students that we do not have to master an infinite number of theories in order to become more theoretically self-conscious. In addition, it permits us more easily to examine the relationship between our often inchoate ideologies, on the one hand, and our perceptions of the historical world, on the other.

Our goal in this book cannot be accomplished without considerable familiarity with and appreciation of the theoretical contributions of scholars in many different fields: anthropology, biology, economics, history, political science, psychology, and sociology. Nevertheless, since most scholars have underestimated the importance of ideology, it seems wisest for us to abandon these disciplinary categories and instead to discuss theories of war in the context of the major Western ideological traditions: conservatism, liberalism, and radicalism. (Please note that we are *not* using these terms in the contemporary sense of their representing attitudes toward change or means of achieving it; nor, for that matter, are we necessarily implying that they stand for "timeless" human points of view.) Our organizational approach thus differs markedly from previous ones, whose basic categories have been disciplinary or topical in perspective.[6] We begin

6. See, for example, Quincy Wright, *A Study of War* (Chicago: University of Chicago Press, 1943, abridged 1964), pp. 103-327; Luther Lee Bernard, *War and Its Causes* (New York: Henry Holt, 1944), pp. 201-438; Waltz, *Man, the State, and War*, pp. 1-15; Donald A. Wells, *The War Myth* (New York: Pegasus, 1967), pp. 171-213; James E. Dougherty and Robert L. Pfaltzgraff, Jr., *Contending Theories of International Relations* (Philadelphia: J. B. Lippincott, 1971), pp. 65-344; Norman Z. Alcock, *The War Disease* (Ontario: Canadian Peace Research Institute, 1972), pp. 6-196; Klaus Jürgen Gantzel, *System und Akteur: Beiträge zur vergleichenden Kriegsursachenforschung* (Düsseldorf: Bertelsmann Universitätsverlag, 1972), pp. 62-72; Bernard Brodie, *War and Politics* (New York: Macmillan, 1973), pp. 276-340; Michael Haas, *International Conflict* (New York: Bobbs-Merrill, 1974), pp. 67-97, 161-184, and 301-323; Robert M. Rood and Charles W. Kegley, Jr., "Explaining War and Conflict: A Review of Contemporary Studies," *Historical Methods Newsletter*, 7 (December 1973), pp. 25-33; Berenice A. Carroll and Clinton F. Fink, "Theories of War Causation: A Matrix for Analysis," in Martin Nettleship, R. Dale Givens, and Anderson Nettleship (eds.), *War, Its Causes and Correlates* (The Hague: Mouton, 1975), pp. 55-71; and

in the first three chapters by surveying and defining these ideological traditions with particular reference to the kinds of theories that each has developed to explain and assess the causes of wars. In Chapters 4 and 5 we examine the ideological and theoretical inclinations (often unconscious or implicit) of a number of leading historians of two major conflicts: World War I and World War II. Finally, in the Epilogue, we discuss the applicability of our categories to other phenomena, we advance some speculations of our own about how war can be explained, and we reassert our plea for a greater effort by historians to carry out comparative studies.

We wish to express our appreciation to those scholars from whose perceptive criticisms and helpful suggestions we have benefited. These include a number of our colleagues in the Department of History at the University of California, Irvine: Professors Kendall Bailes, Richard Frank, Karl Hufbauer, Jon Jacobson, Michael Johnson, Arthur Marder, Patricia O'Brien, Mark Poster, and Jon Wiener, as well as the graduate students in History and Theory, especially David Romagnolo. In addition, we thank historians and social scientists at other institutions: Professors Joyce Appleby of San Diego State University, Kent Beck of Pennsylvania State University, Michael Haas of the University of Hawaii, Robert Jervis of the University of California, Los Angeles, Alan Lawson of Boston College, David Levering of the California State University at Pomona, Melvin Small of Wayne State University, Richard C. Snyder of the Mershon Center of Ohio State University, and Dina A. Zinnes of Indiana University. Natalie Korp typed more drafts than we care to remember, but always with great competence.

Lancelot L. Farrar, Jr. (ed.), *War: A Historical, Political, and Social Study* (Santa Barbara: ABC-Clio Press, 1978).

CHAPTER ONE

Conservative Ideology and Theory about the Causes of War

THE CONSERVATIVE TRADITION

Modern conservatism as an ideology emerged in response to the increasing social change and resulting instability of the Western world in the period since the Renaissance. In particular it developed as a reaction on the part of political and social elites against the Commercial and French Revolutions and the ideas stimulated by those momentous events —individualism, notions of equality, faith in reason and science, belief in progress. The conservatives' opponents, the bourgeois "liberal" champions of a "new" society, waged a relentless campaign on behalf of the individual's emancipation from the constricting fetters of age-old privilege and tradition. Conservatives, in their carefully constructed response, stressed the primacy of community and the importance of preserving the traditional institutional order, the "order bequeathed by history."[1]

1. See Robert Nisbet, *The Sociological Tradition* (New York: Basic Books, 1966), p. 12. For somewhat different accounts of the origins of modern conservatism, see Karl Mannheim, "Conservative Thought," in Kurt H. Wolff (ed.), *From Karl Mannheim* (New York: Oxford University Press, 1971), pp. 132-222; and Samuel P. Huntington, "Conservatism as an Ideology," *American Political Science Review*, 51 (June 1957), pp. 454-473. Useful anthologies are Peter Viereck (ed.), *Conservatism from John Adams to Churchill* (Princeton: Princeton University Press 1956); and Robert Schuettinger (ed.), *The Conservative Tradition in European Thought* (New York: Capricorn, 1971).

To be sure, conservatives were not always in full agreement (particularly as the rate of historical change accelerated) as to which of the great traditions were most basic or as to how these might be fortified. They often disagreed, for example, about the role of the increasingly successful nation-state in preserving various values and structures. Conservatives such as Francis Hotman (1524-1590) and Juan de Mariana (1536-1624), who saw the centralizing king and state as a threat to aristocratic power and inherited privilege, linked themselves to medieval notions of "balanced" and decentralized government.[2] Others like Jean Bodin (1530-1596) and Sir Robert Filmer (ca. 1590-1653) were persuaded that disintegration of the earlier synthesis had proceeded to the point that only a strong monarch could keep things in proper order.[3] Still, all conservatives were as one in their emphasis on the dangers which lay in an unstructured and undisciplined society.

Thus conservative ideology begins with the bold assertion that there is a social reality and a social good prior to and greater than privately determined individual rights and individual goods. Edmund Burke (1729-1797), the eighteenth-century British critic of the French Revolution and perhaps the best known of all conservatives, had a conception of the individual's proper relationship to the social order that was in marked contrast to that of the liberals. Possessing more *skepticism* than they *about the perfectability of man*, Burke rejected the desirability, even the possibility, of the "autonomous" individual so central to liberal theory. Burke's sense of the "connectedness" of individuals, of the network of social obligations that binds

2. See George H. Sabine, *A History of Political Theory* (London: Harrap, 1948), pp. 320-333. A preference for "balanced" or "limited" government is also apparent in such later conservatives as David Hume and other celebrants of Britain's Glorious Revolution. See Sheldon S. Wolin, "Hume and Conservatism," *American Political Science Review*, 48 (December 1954), pp. 999-1016. See also Huntington, "Conservatism as an Ideology," pp. 463-464.
3. Sabine, *A History of Political Theory*, pp. 340-353, 434-437.

men together and strengthens them, is a basic theme of
conservative thought.

Society, according to Burke, is a partnership, but it is a
partnership "not only between those who are living, but
between those who are living, those who are dead, and those
who are to be born. . . ."[4] The social cement for this partnership was not human love, nor even a sense of human
fraternity, but rather esteem, deference, awe, and respect.
This reverence for "the great primeval contract of eternal
society" led Burke, as it has led subsequent conservatives, to
prefer tradition over innovation, experience over experi-
ment, stability over change. Thus the *feeling of belonging to
a social group* is closely related to *respect for the past* for
Burke and his successors.

In addition to these beliefs in human fallibility and in
community and tradition, there are several other important
elements of conservative thought. One of these has involved
the problem of traditional authority and its continued
erosion. For not only has the loss of traditional community
become obvious during the last two hundred years; so also
has the loss of established authority—that authority related
to immediately mutual function and association, to those
patriarchal, personal, and ritualized bonds deeply enmeshed
in a culture, to those relationships of familiarity and respect,
duty and allegiance, that, working together, obviate the
need for military and political force or administrative
bureaucracy.

In the conservative's perception, the new social reality of
the eighteenth and nineteenth centuries was one in which men
were becoming separated from traditional authorities and
were thereby losing their accustomed reference points. The

4. Edmund Burke, *Reflections on the Revolution in France*, bound
with Thomas Paine, *The Rights of Man* (New York: Dolphin Books, 1961),
p. 110. On Burke, see Carl Cone, *Burke and the Nature of Politics*
(Lexington: University of Kentucky Press, 1960-1964); Russell Kirk, *Edmund Burke: A Genius Reconsidered* (New Rochelle, N.Y.: Arlington
House, 1967); and Isaac Kramnick, *The Rage of Edmund Burke* (New
York: Basic Books, 1977).

French aristocrat Alexis de Tocqueville (1805-1859) effectively expressed this concern: "In our days men see that constituted powers are crumbling down on every side; they see all ancient authority dying out, all ancient barriers tottering to their fall, and the judgment of the wisest is troubled at the sight. . . ."[5] Thus, the longstanding prestige of the patriarchal family, the guild, the town, and the church was being destroyed by an increase both of individualism and of distant political power. Moreover, according to conservative analysis, the atomized individual, torn from his traditional community by economic and social forces beyond his control, was ill equipped to manage the centralized power of the new democratic states. A substitution of majoritarianism for traditional authority was vehemently attacked, for example, by Sir Henry Maine (1822-1888):

On the complex questions of politics, which are calculated in themselves to task to the utmost all the powers of the strongest minds, . . . the common determination of a multitude is a chimerical assumption; and indeed, if it were really possible to extract an opinion upon them from a great mass of men, and to shape the administrative and legislative acts of a State upon this opinion as a sovereign command, it is probable that the most ruinous blunders would be committed, and all social progress would be arrested.[6]

Such thoughts point up a fourth element in the conservative tradition: a *belief in the desirability of hierarchy and differentiated status*. This of course follows plausibly from pessimistic assumptions about human nature. Indeed, just as conservatives have tended to turn to the community and to the past to counterbalance the individual's frailty, so they have called upon a permanently experienced leadership (or, as Alexander Hamilton put it, the "rich, the well-born, and the able") in hopes of finding enough self-discipline and

5. Alexis de Tocqueville, *Democracy in America*, 2 vols. (New York: Vintage Books, 1945; first published in 1835 and 1840), Vol. II, p. 333. On Tocqueville, see Marvin Zetterbaum, *Tocqueville and the Problem of Democracy* (Stanford, Calif.: Stanford University Press, 1967).
6. Sir Henry Sumner Maine, *Popular Government: Four Essays* (London: John Murray, 1885), pp. 88-89.

wisdom to control man's generally too passionate nature. Such an arrangement was qualified and delimited in traditional, pre-democratic, pre-industrial society by its organic nature: i.e., by the mutual responsibility and duty practiced by the three distinct estates (aristocracy, priesthood, and peasantry); by the variety of connections that united each of these groups; and by the religiously sanctioned "chain of all the members of the community, from the peasant to the King" (in Tocqueville's words). The division of labor intrinsic to this notion of hierarchy, where the propertied elites command, and the masses obey, appeared to early conservatives as an inevitable part of an eternal, unchangeable social order.

In a democratic society, however, this "chain" is broken, for, since the citizens have no "natural" ties to one another, the principle of hierarchy is denied. The function of hierarchy is obviously at odds with the role of "the people"; the principle of majoritarianism strikes at the heart of hierarchical authority.[7] There is also a serious conflict between the power of centralized, rationalized bureaucracy in the modern nation-state and the preservation of private control over fundamental social actions (as Tocqueville, and later, Ferdinand Tönnies, Max Weber, and Robert Michels so clearly demonstrated.)[8]

The new society, according to conservative observations, is characterized not by the strengthening of social classes (as radicals would later assert), but rather by the replacement of earlier "layers" with more mobile status groups and status-seeking individuals. Sociologist Robert Nisbet asks the central quesitons of this historic debate between conservatives and their radical opponents in these terms:

7. One of the most important parts of the *philosophes'* attack on traditional society was their critique of hierarchy and stratification. See particularly Jean Jacques Rousseau's *Discourse on the Origin of Inequality* (New York: E. P. Dutton, 1941; originally published in 1754).

8. On this see Seymour Drescher, *Dilemmas of Democracy: Tocqueville and Modernization* (Pittsburgh, Pa.: Pittsburgh University Press, 1968).

Was [this new society, based as it was] on the imperious if uncertain and often misled will of the masses, dominated by new structures of administrative power and flooded by new forms of wealth, [and] driven by novel and incessant pressures for educational, religious, and social equality . . . , was this society to be, as had been all previous forms of society, organized primarily in terms of class layers . . . ? Or, in sharp contrast, could the acids of modernity be seen working in as destructive a fashion upon the bases of social class . . . as they were upon village community, extended family, and the whole network of moral cultural relations that had also been born in the pre-capitalist, pre-democratic, pre-rationalist age?[9]

The answers to these crucial questions tended to follow ideological lines. There was, in other words, a direct correlation between the ways in which one approached the related issues of community, authority, and stratification. Conservatives (following the insights of Tocqueville) held that social class and authority were even less in evidence in the modern age than in earlier ones, while radicals (in the tradition of Karl Marx) stressed that the new bourgeois class had usurped the position of the aristocracy. Both sides agreed that one significant consequence of economic and political modernization was the destruction of the traditional social hierarchy. Conservatives deplored this fact; liberals and radicals applauded it.

A fifth tenet of conservative ideology, related to the respect for tradition, is an insistence on the *wisdom of historical variety.* This insistence was originally an aspect of the Romantic reaction to the "liberal" Enlightenment of the eighteenth century, and it developed in conjunction with a continental attack on English and French liberalism. As one historian of wit has described it, east of the Rhine there occurred a vigorous and understandable rejection of the British and French tendency to take their own peculiar ways and universalize and generalize from them in the name of reason. Georg W. F. Hegel (1770-1831) and other conservative thinkers now came close to an assertion that "whatever

9. Nisbet, *The Sociological Tradition*, pp. 180-181.

is, is right" in their willingness to attribute a touch of divine justification to particular social and national groupings. They were well on their way toward that affiliation with nationalism that has become so typical of modern conservatism.[10]

Such nationalist inclinations, however, did not preclude the existence of a continuing strain of *anti-statism* in modern conservatism—a revulsion against the centralized, bureaucratic state and an insistent denial that the state is a legitimate agency for social action. Particularly in twentieth-century Britain, conservatives have come to argue that every effort ought to be made to accomplish common social goals without the government's intervention. One ironic result is that, in this way, pessimism about mankind has often led conservatives into alliance with (or absorption by) liberal groups which oppose governmental activity out of an optimism about humanity. On the other hand, in those areas like the European continent where conservatives have tended to recognize the advantages of strong central authority, another irony developed, for here the road was open to cooperation with the fascists, who would ultimately overturn all tradition in the name of order.[11] Conservatism, like

10. Sabine, *A History of Political Theory*, pp. 522-561. For the controversy that has long raged over the implications of Hegel's ideas, see Walter Kaufmann (ed.), *Hegel's Political Philosophy* (New York: Atherton, 1970). See also Shlomo Avineri, *Hegel's Theory of the Modern State* (Cambridge: Cambridge University Press, 1972).

11. The reader will note that there exists another line of thought, to the right of the great conservative tradition, which might be loosely called the "Fascist" tradition. This is largely a nineteenth- and twentieth-century phenomenon, decidedly anti-intellectual in tone, and characterized by racism, extreme nationalism, authoritarianism, and willingness to employ force. There is thus a kind of Manichaean and angry quality about this "radical right," that is, a readiness to see the international scene in terms of "good and bad," with one's own nation in the role of a single-minded and avenging Providence. Though in times of peace its doctrines are championed by only a compulsive minority, in the heat of war its attitudes and ideas often come to be widely accepted. In general, however, the theory produced by this tradition with regard to the causes of war is underdeveloped and fragmentary, assuming the inevitability of conflict and glorifying violence and domination. On the Fascist and proto-Fascist

the other ideological traditions, has been steadily plagued with the problem of how to cope with political power.

Thus a number of emphases can be identified in that inter-related set of beliefs that we call the conservative tradition. Starting from a doctrine of *man as a creature of only modest capabilities,* conservatives tend to stress the wisdom of his *dependence on the historical community,* that is, a group that includes all our ancestors and descendants as well as ourselves. Put another way, the implication is that *a decent respect for, and willingness to learn from, other generations requires us not to deviate unnecessarily from the procedures that have worked* in the past. Moreover, it is sensible, when the dangers of confusion are so very great, to *entrust leadership* (and accompanying status) *to that elite which has demonstrated its capacities* through practice. If the people will stand behind this "true" aristocracy of talent and experience, individuals and nations will achieve the *freedom to act and live in accord with their own traditions.* As for the state, conservatives have been ambivalent as to whether the exigencies of the historical moment require that leadership seize and exercise its power or simply keep it to a minimum.

CONSERVATIVE THEORY ABOUT CONFLICT AND WAR

In considering the ideas of conservatives about international conflict, it is useful to recall Edmund Burke's basic indictment of the revolutionary leaders of eighteenth-century France: that they had committed the disastrous, the

tradition, see Hans Rogger and Eugen Weber (eds.), *The European Right: A Historical Profile* (Berkeley: University of California Press, 1965); John Weiss, *The Fascist Tradition: Radical Right-Wing Extremism in Modern Europe* (New York: Harper and Row, 1967); and Daniel Bell (ed.), *The New American Right* (New York: 1955; enlarged and revised, 1962). See also Luther Lee Bernard, *War and Its Causes* (New York: Henry Holt, 1944), pp. 141-164; and Ole R. Holsti, "The Study of International Politics Makes Strange Bedfellows: Theories of the Radical Right and Radical Left," *American Political Science Review,* 68 (March 1974), pp. 217-242.

unforgivable error of attempting to create a society based on abstract principles that bore no necessary relation to the history, traditions, social structure, or culture of the French people. For Burke, politics had to be experiential, not deductive. Effective use over time was the only justification for a particular institution or policy. Liberal assertions about "natural laws" or "natural rights" were worse than useless, for they mistakenly assumed that man can be abstracted from his social context and that one can discuss rights to the exclusion of duties.

These Burkean attitudes provide an interesting clue as to why over the years conservatives have tended not to theorize about the cause of conflict and war. From the point of view of the typical conservative, it is almost impossible to actualize theoretical knowledge. We may visualize a more perfect society, even desire it, but human nature is not really capable of moving from the imperfect present to the social ideal. This conservative skepticism regarding the usefulness of theory is strikingly different from the Marxist reliance on "praxis," according to which theory and action are mutually reinforcing. Indeed, unlike radicals, conservatives often deny the rationality of the historical process as well as distinguish theory from practice. Such a view undoubtedly accounts for the fact that there are so few examples in historical literature of conservative utopias.

If conservative theories of international relations and war are therefore somewhat fewer in number and less highly developed than their liberal and radical counterparts, it is nevertheless apparent that there are at least two distinct strains of conservative thought about the subject: one which presupposes that individuals and nations are basically aggressive in behavior, as animals are often thought to be, and a second which suggests that wars result when nations lose their internal discipline and order, or when international hierarchies break down. Both kinds of theory obviously proceed from the assumption that the masses of mankind are driven *not* by considerations of the general welfare, but by ignorance, emotion, and selfishness. Both tend to view war as a natural, almost inevitable, and certainly frequent social occurrence. Proponents of the second theory are clearly somewhat more optimistic, since they admit the possibility that conflict can be reduced if trained elites are in a position to counteract the natural impulses of the people. This group is also more common historically, since only at times of severe fatalism has mankind been able to dispense with significant avenues of hope. But in any case it is notable that both conservative approaches put great emphasis upon the indispensable role which power plays in the maintenance of peace. Only a clear and decisive balance of power, it is suggested, can keep man's animalistic and anarchic tendencies in check. In national affairs this force should be in the hands of established authorities; in international affairs in the hands of the leading nations. Otherwise, according to these "realists," there will be violence and/or war on either the national or international level, or both, until a preponderant power is reestablished.

Individuals and Nations as Animals

The idea that a human is a dependent creature, vulnerable to baser instincts and hardly a step above the rest of the animal world is a concept that has been present in our culture a long time, going back in one of its versions at least as far as early Christian doctrines of original sin. "But I see another law in my members," said Saint Paul, "warring against the law of my mind and bringing me into captivity to the law of sin which is in my members."[12] Or again, in the words of the Anglican confession of sin: "We have left undone those things which we ought to have done; And we have done those things which we ought not to have done; And there is no health in us."[13]

The implications of such pessimism for a theory of war

12. Romans 7:18-23.
13. See the "General Confession" in the orders of morning and evening prayer in *The Book of Common Prayer*, published first in 1549.

were articulated by Saint Augustine (354-430) as early as the fifth century. Writing during the period in which the disintegration of the Roman Empire was becoming evident, Augustine developed a heavily deterministic theory which explained conflict as either (1) arising from "human passion" and unregulated desire, or (2) occurring in obedience to the will of God in order to "rebuke, or humble, or crush the pride of man." In either case Augustine was convinced that war fulfilled the useful purpose of reminding man just how weak and dependent he actually is.[14]

In the modern era one of the earliest and most original of the conservative commentators on war was the Englishman Thomas Hobbes (1588-1679). Clearly more secular than Augustine, Hobbes was similar to the theologian not only in writing during an age of great social turmoil (the English revolution) but also in his feelings that "the bonds of words are too weak to bridle man's ambition, avarice, anger, and other passions, without the fear of some coercive power." Robbed by his lack of religious faith of any significant trust in God's responsibility, Hobbes sought his solution to the dilemma of man's lusts in the power of the earthly ruler. To fortify what he called that "great Leviathan, or rather (to speak more reverently), . . . that Mortal God" (i.e., the state), every man must be "willing, when others are so too, as far forth . . . for peace, and defence of himself as he shall think it necessary, to lay down his right to all things. . . ."[15]

Hobbes is frequently contrasted with his countryman and

14. Saint Augustine, *The City of God* (New York: Random House, 1950), Book III, Sections 4 and 30, Book XIX, paragraph 7. With regard to the second category Augustine introduced the notion of the "just war," which subsequent Christians extended. On this, and on the ambivalence of the Christian tradition with regard to war, see Herbert A. Deane, *The Political and Social ideas of St. Augustine* (New York: Columbia University Press, 1963), pp. 154-171; Roland H. Bainton, *Christian Attitudes Toward War and Peace* (New York: Abingdon, 1960), pp. 53-121; and Donald A. Wells, *The War Myth* (New York: Pegasus, 1967), pp. 32-39, 129-169.

15. Thomas Hobbes, *Leviathan* (Oxford: Clarendon Press, 1909; originally published in 1651), Chaps. 14 and 17.

younger contemporary, John Locke (1632-1704), and for good reason. Whereas Locke was to become a basic source of liberal thought, Hobbes, like Niccolò Machiavelli (1469-1527) before him, became an inspiration for those who wished to analyze the uses of political power unconstrained by matters of sentiment or morality. Though both Hobbes and Locke hypothesized a state of nature in which men had existed prior to establishing agreements, or contracts, among themselves, for Hobbes such a situation had approximated a war of all against all, while for Locke the state of nature had constituted a mere inconvenience. It therefore followed that for Hobbes, in contrast to Locke, almost nothing could justify the overthrow of a monarch and the return of mankind to the state of nature. He took this position knowing full well that on the international level a state of nature continued to exist and could not be escaped: "For the state of commonwealths considered in themselves, is natural, that is to say, hostile. Neither if they cease from fighting, is it therefore to be called peace; but rather a breathing time. . . ."[16]

By the nineteenth century a more "scientific" set of ideas had become available to those who wished to tie humans to the animal (and therefore, presumably, more ruthless) side of their inherited nature. Though Charles Darwin's *Origin of Species* (1859) did not assume an explicit position on

16. Thomas Hobbes, *De Cive, or The Citizen* (New York: Appleton-Century-Crofts, 1949; originally published in 1642), Chap. 13. It should be noted that Hobbes was far from an ordinary conservative in his day. Indeed, his materialism, skepticism of tradition, and willingness to base political obligations on self-interest meant that he had many affinities with liberalism. What persuades us to leave him in the conservative tradition is his severe pessimism about human nature, which brings him to conclude that in the absence of sovereign power men and nations would be at each other's throats. On this, see Keith Brown (ed.), *Hobbes Studies* (Oxford: Blackwell, 1965); and Richard H. Cox, *Locke on War and Peace* (Oxford: Clarendon Press, 1960), pp. 142-147. Another early modern figure who could be offered as an example of the more pessimistic kind of conservatism is Benedict de Spinoza; in this regard see Kenneth N. Waltz, *Man, the State, and War* (New York: Columbia University Press, 1959), pp. 22-30, 162.

political and social issues, this did not prevent intellectuals of the period from reading a wide variety of optimistic and pessimistic implications into his theory. On occasion (as with Herbert Spencer or William Graham Sumner) "Social Darwinism" became a kind of promise that, no matter what the short-run difficulties, the destiny of the human race would be one of steady improvement and progress. In the hands of other interpreters (often called "Malthusians"), however, the same doctrines were used to picture an inescapable and inevitably gruesome struggle in which only a few of the very fittest survived. Toward the end of the century it became less common to apply Darwinian ideas to domestic situations (as in applauding competition among economic units) and more typical to utilize them in description of international and interracial relations. Thus in the work of conservative theorists like Count Arthur de Gobineau (1816-1882) and Houston Stewart Chamberlain (1855-1927), there appeared a view in which nations and races, like organisms, were constantly forced to battle each other for survival. As the American admiral Alfred Thayer Mahan (1840-1914) expressed it: "All around us now is strife; 'the struggle for life,' 'the race of life,' are phrases so familiar that we do not feel their significance till we stop to think about them. Everywhere nation is arrayed against nation; our own no less than others."[17]

We see this same sense of peril, if in somewhat different guise, in the writings of the psychologist Sigmund Freud (1856-1939). Committed as he was to the notion that the inmost essence of human nature consists of elemental instincts among which a destructive drive figures promi-

17. Richard Hofstadter, *Social Darwinism in American Thought* (Boston: Beacon Press, 1955), p. 188. Hofstadter's work is still the best on this subject, but see also Paul F. Boller, Jr., *American Thought in Transition: The Impact of Evolutionary Naturalism, 1865-1900* (Chicago: Rand McNally, 1969); and Pitirim Sorokin, *Contemporary Sociological Theories* (New York: Harper and Brothers, 1928), Chap. 6. It should be noted that the racist side of Darwinian arguments feeds into the Fascist tradition (see note 11).

nently, Freud concluded in a famous essay of 1915 that "war cannot be abolished; [since] so long as the conditions of existence among nations are so different and their mutual repulsion so violent, there are bound to be wars." Later, in his old age, Freud was to revise this opinion, writing to Albert Einstein in 1932 of his hope that culture could be structured so as to meet man's inner needs and thereby avoid war. There were two ongoing developments that the psychologist now found particularly promising: "firstly, a strengthening of the intellect, which tends to master our instinctual life, and secondly, an introversion of the aggressive impulse, with all its consequent benefits and perils." Almost unconsciously, then, Freud was moving toward that position which has become characteristic of present-day neo-Freudians (e.g., Erich Fromm, Erik Erikson), playing down the role of inherited tendencies and emphasizing the shaping power of society. Nevertheless, he left a vigorous legacy of skepticism about the extent to which individuals and nations genuinely and wholeheartedly desire peace.[18]

In our own era much of Freud's original pessimism and doubt has reappeared in the conclusions of certain students of animal behavior. The best known of these scientists, Konrad Lorenz (1903-   ), is, like Freud, a physician and Viennese by birth. On the basis of his observations, primarily with birds and fish, Lorenz contends that there is an aggressive instinct embedded in the phylogenetic structure of all species. If humans and the lower animals had not developed mechanisms that inhibit fighting—mechanisms like status systems, the love bond, and ritualization—their very survival would have come into question. As it is, according to Lorenz, the inhibitory controls imposed on aggression both through natural selection and through

18. Freud's two pieces on war (of 1915 and 1932) are in James Strachey (ed.), *The Standard Edition of the Complete Psychological Works of Sigmund Freud*, 24 vols. (London: Hogarth Press, 1953-1974), Vols. 14 and 22. See also Paul Roazen, *Freud: Political and Social Thought* (New York: Alfred A. Knopf, 1968), pp. 193-212; and Franco Fornari, *The Psychoanalysis of War* (New York: Anchor Books, 1974).

cultural processes frequently fail under the pressure of
events. In Lorenz's own words:

> It is not so much the sudden, one-time great temptation that makes
> human morality break down but the effect of any prolonged
> situation that exerts an increasing drain on the compensatory
> power of morality. Hunger, anxiety, the necessity to make difficult
> decisions, overwork, hopelessness and the like all have the effect of
> sapping moral energy and, in the long run, making it break down.
> Anyone who has had the opportunity to observe men under this
> kind of strain, for example in war or in prisoner-of-war camps,
> knows how unpredictably and suddenly moral decompensation
> sets in.

Thus, when the aggression instinct is dammed up too long,
or when the controls break down, any animal or group of
animals can turn violently on its own species.[19]

An interesting if not entirely surprising variation on
Lorenz's views is provided by the anthropologist Sherwood
Washburn (1911-   ). Unwilling to accept the assertion that
man is innately aggressive, Washburn contends that the
problem actually lies in the "carnivorous psychology" which
man has developed, largely as a result of having lived 99
percent of his earthly history as a hunter and predator. "For
at least 300,000 years (perhaps twice that)," he says, "carnivorous curiosity and aggression have been added to the
inquisitiveness and dominance striving of the ape." Washburn goes on to add:

> The extent to which the biological bases for killing have been
> incorporated into human psychology may be measured by the ease
> with which boys can be interested in hunting, fishing, fighting, and
> games of war. It is not that these behaviors are inevitable, but they
> are easily learned, satisfying, and have been socially rewarded in
> most cultures.[20]

19. Konrad Lorenz, *On Aggression* (London: Methuen, 1966), pp. 221-
222. For an interesting set of rebuttals to Lorenz, see M. F. Ashley
Montagu (ed.), *Man and Aggression* (New York: Oxford University Press,
1968). See also Erich Fromm, *The Anatomy of Human Destructiveness*
(New York: Holt, Rinehart, and Winston, 1973). For a contemporary view
similar to Lorenz's, see Robert Ardrey, *The Territorial Imperative* (New
York: Atheneum, 1966).
20. See Sherwood L. Washburn and C. S. Lancaster, "The Evolution of

Wars are therefore not engendered by our social system, nor by misperceptions and misunderstandings among men, but instead by destructive forces deeply ingrained in the attitudes of the race. Like others on the farther reaches of pessimism, Washburn seems to imply that mankind is fortunate to escape with only intermittent war.

The Nation and/or International Affairs as Disciplined or Undisciplined

A more sophisticated, elaborate, and perhaps self-serving version of the conservative perspective on conflict is provided by theorists who argue that war can be avoided only if society and state and international relations are organized in proper hierarchical (and preferably traditional) fashion. As we have noted earlier, it is not so much that the holders of this view possess any more elevated estimate of human nature than do those who see a world of tooth and claw. Rather, those who espouse hierarchy and tradition argue merely that the flaws inherent in humanity are minimized when every person and nation knows his (its) place in the social and political order, and when rulers and leading countries have been schooled to guard against their own weaknesses. This does not exclude the possibility that a ruler or dominant power might occasionally want to utilize war for reasons of state, as a means to accomplish a specific, limited end. Nevertheless, the need for such wars should be relatively slight if power is securely in the hands of the "natural" leaders (in both domestic and international senses). It is when this order disintegrates or breaks down, as for example, through ineptitude on the part of leadership or

Hunting," in Richard B. Lee and Irving Devore (eds.), *Man the Hunter* (Chicago: Aldine, 1966), pp. 293-303. For other treatments of violence as a "learned" behavior, see David N. Daniels, Marshall F. Gilula, and Frank Ochberg (eds.), *Violence and the Struggle for Existence* (Boston: Little, Brown, 1970); and Albert Bandura, *Aggression: A Social Learning Analysis* (Englewood Cliffs, N.J.: Prentice-Hall, 1973). See also Lionel Tiger and Robin Fox, *The Imperial Animal* (New York: Holt, Rinehart and Winston, 1971).

through agitation on the part of popular demagogues, that the dangers of violence become the greatest. It is then that rulers or ruling nations may not be able to control the aggressive impulses of their followers or may find it necessary to go to war in order to reestablish acceptance of discipline.

Such, briefly, is the core of a perspective which is as old or older than the nation-state itself. Even in ancient times, Livy (59 B.C.-A.D. 17) could speak approvingly of the Roman Senate having "ordered an immediate raising of troops and a general mobilization on the largest possible scale . . . , in the hope that the revolutionary proposals which the tribunes were bringing forward might be forgotten in the bustle and excitement of three imminent campaigns. . . ."[21] In the early modern era Martin Luther (1483-1546) strongly echoed such sentiments in asserting that war might be necessary in crises of authority to restore the health of the body politic.[22] Later, Thomas Hobbes contended that a foreign war should be much preferred to civil conflict because kings could "uphold thereby the industry of their subjects."[23]

Conservatives of this kind have not always blamed the people at large, however, for the breakdown or decline in a nation's discipline. To be sure, the presumption has generally been that the ruler and his men (administrators and military leaders) are more dependable than the commoners (though Hobbes' admonitions against "unnecessary wars" undertaken out of ambition or for revenge or fame indicate that not even rulers could be trusted fully). Yet often conservatives have worried not so much about the people as a whole as about certain elements within the body politic that, through their perversity or confusion, have threatened or actually undermined the traditional order of society.

21. Livy, *The Early History of Rome* (Baltimore: Penguin Books, 1960), p. 253. On this, see R. I. Frank, "The Dangers of Peace," *Prudentia*, 8 (May 1976), pp. 1-7.

22. Bernard, *War and Its Causes*, pp. 130-132. See also Sabine, *A History of Political Theory*, pp. 304-310.

23. Hobbes, *Leviathan*, Chap. 13.

Moreover, conservative observers have frequently seen this sort of trouble as being further advanced in other nation-states than in their own. Edmund Burke, for example, viewed revolutionary France as a country that had fallen under the control of a group within its population enamoured of "pernicious principles":

That faction is the evil spirit that possesses the body of France,—that informs it as a soul,—that stamps upon its ambition, and upon all its pursuits, a characteristic mark, which strongly distinguishes them from the same general passions and the same general views in other men and in other communities. It is a spirit which inspires into them a new, pernicious, a desolating activity.

To Burke the threat from revolutionary France to the rest of Europe was so severe that war on the part of England could be and was a purely defensive action:

It is a war between the partisans of the ancient civil, moral, and political order of Europe against a sect of fanatical and ambitious atheists which means to change them all.

Nor did Burke believe that the issues between France and the rest of the world could be compromised:

I never thought we could make peace with the [French] system; because it was not for the sake of an object we pursued in rivalry with each other, but with the system itself that we were at war. As I understood the matter, we were at war, not with its conduct, but with its existence,—convinced that its existence and its hostility were the same.[24]

Though Burke was not willing to glorify war as such (he spoke of it as an "inevitable evil" that man could only hope to "mitigate"), there has been a tendency for representatives of this tradition to gravitate toward the justification of war as a positive good. Thus the idealist philosopher, G. W. F.

24. Burke, "Letters on a Regicide Peace," written in 1795-1796 and published in W. J. Bate (ed.), *Edmund Burke: Selected Works* (New York: Modern Library, 1960), pp. 479-482. Though this view bears certain similarities to what we shall identify in Chapter 2 as liberal "group conflict" theory about war, it should be emphasized that Burke, unlike group conflict thinkers, tends to see a "faction" (a group held together by ideas *and* interests) as necessarily a danger to society and peace.

26   CONSERVATIVE IDEOLOGY AND THEORY

Hegel, after pointing out that "successful wars have checked domestic unrest and consolidated the power of the state at home," went on to assert that "just as the blowing of the winds preserves the sea from the foulness which would be the result of a prolonged calm, so also corruption in nations would be the product of prolonged, let alone 'perpetual,' peace."[25] The Swiss historian Jacob Burckhardt (1818-1897) was equally emphatic on this point.

> Lasting peace not only leads to enervation; it permits the rise of a mass of precarious, fear-ridden, distressful lives which would not have survived without it and which nevertheless clamor for their "rights," cling somehow to existence, bar the way to genuine ability, thicken the air and as a whole degrade the nation's blood. War restores real ability to a place of honor. As for these precarious existences, war may at least reduce them to silence.[26]

Later in the nineteenth century, as Europe and America reeled under the impact of industrialization and social change, many individuals with conservative or aristocratic predilections also came to appreciate war as an instrument for keeping reformers or grasping commercial classes from destroying the virtues of discipline and destabilizing the world. As one Texas congressman put it to Secretary of State Richard Olney at the time of the 1895 Venezuela crisis:

> Why, Mr. Secretary, just think of how angry the anarchistic, socialistic, and populistic boil appears on our political surface and who knows how deep its roots extend or ramify? One cannon shot across the bow of a British boat in defense of this principle [the Monroe Doctrine] will knock more pus out of it than would suffice to innoculate and corrupt [sic] our people for the next two centuries.[27]

A few months after this, Assistant Secretary of the Navy Theodore Roosevelt (1858-1919) bemoaned the fact that the

25. Georg W. F. Hegel, *Philosophy of Right* (Oxford: Clarendon Press, 1942), p. 210. In this passage, first published in 1821, he recapitulates ideas about war which he had stated as early as 1802-1803.

26. Jacob Burckhardt, *Force and Freedom: Reflections on History* (New York: Pantheon, 1943), p. 261. The passage dates from 1868-1869.

27. Quoted in Richard Hofstadter, *The Paranoid Style in American Politics and Other Essays* (New York: Vintage, 1967), p. 154.

activities of the money-grubbing American bourgeoisie were "producing a flabby, timid type of character which eats away the great fighting qualities of our race":

There are higher things in life than the soft and easy enjoyment of material comfort. It is through strife, or the readiness for strife, that a nation must win greatness. . . . A rich nation which is slothful, timid, or unwieldy is an easy prey for any people which still retain those most valuable of qualities, the martial virtues.[28]

The German general Helmuth von Moltke (1800-1892), victor of the Franco-Prussian War, had earlier had similar reactions:

[War] fosters the noblest virtues of man, courage, self-denial, obedience to duty, and the spirit of sacrifice; the soldier gives his life. Without war the world would stagnate and sink into materialism.[29]

Meanwhile, more responsible conservatives continued to oppose violence and war in general and to demand a leader-

28. Theodore Roosevelt, *Works*, 20 vols. (New York: Charles Scribner's Sons, 1926), Vol. XVIII, pp. 66-67. There is an excellent discussion of Roosevelt's and similar points of view in John P. Mallan, "Roosevelt, Brooks Adams, and Lea: The Warrior Critique of the Business Civilization," *American Quarterly*, 8 (Fall 1956), pp. 216-229. It is interesting to note that William James, though putting himself squarely in the "antimilitarist party," found himself agreeing with much of what Roosevelt said: "A permanently successful peace-economy cannot be a simple pleasure-economy. In the more or less socialistic future towards which mankind seems drifting we must still subject ourselves to those severities which answer to our real position upon this only partly hospitable globe. We must make new energies and hardihoods continue the manliness to which the military mind so faithfully clings." From William James, "The Moral Equivalent of War" (1910), in John J. McDermott (ed.), *The Writings of William James* (New York: Random House, 1967), p. 668.
29. Helmuth von Moltke to J. K. Bluntschli, December 11, 1880, in Thomas H. Holland (ed.), *Letters on War and Neutrality* (New York: Longmans Green, 1909), p. 25. It should be apparent that by emphasizing the benefits to be derived from war, thinkers like Hegel, Roosevelt, and von Moltke are touching upon the borders of the tradition of the radical right. Indeed, many interpreters have seen them as among the progenitors of modern Fascism. However, as long as such individuals treat war more as a historical necessity than as a glorious achievement in itself, we believe that they are more correctly placed within the conservative tradition. Admittedly, it is a fine line.

Voting leads to exacs (handwritten marginalia)

ship strong enough to avoid having to "use" force or succumb to popular pressure for it. In accord with such beliefs the British statesman Benjamin Disraeli (1804-1881) spoke out in 1859 against enlarging the national electorate, arguing that, with democracy, "you will in due season reap the fruits of such united influence. You will in due season have wars entered into from passion and not from reason; and you will in due season submit to peace ignominiously sought and ignominiously obtained, which will diminish your authority and perhaps endanger your independence."[30] In a subsequent generation Winston Churchill (1874-1965), though understandably more tolerant than Disraeli of equalitarian beliefs, seems to have harbored similar doubts about the capacities of the people. "Democracy," he maintained in 1901, "is more vindictive than Cabinets. The wars of peoples will be more terrible than those of kings."[31]

Contemporary conservatives (being somewhat less traditionalist and more liberal than heretofore) are less inclined to blame the populace for war than were their predecessors, but they remain committed to the necessity of domestic order and dominating, cautious leadership. Moreover, for the achievement of peace, they place considerable emphasis on the need for a clearly defined hierarchy, or at least a well established equilibrium of international power. The so-called "Realist" school of American foreign policy, for

30. Benjamin Disraeli, Speech in the House of Commons, March 31, 1859, in Montagu Corry (ed.), *Parliamentary Reform* (London: Longmans Green, 1867) and in Schuettinger, *The Conservative Tradition in European Thought*, pp. 236-237. Another representative of the cautious approach was the Austrian statesman Prince Clemens von Metternich. See Henry Kissinger, "The Conservative Dilemma: Reflections on the Political Thought of Metternich," *American Political Science Review*, 48 (December 1954), pp. 1017-1030

31. Winston Churchill, Speech in the House of Commons, May 13, 1901, in Martin Gilbert (ed.), *Churchill* (Englewood Cliffs, N.J.: Prentice-Hall, 1967), pp. 21-22. See also Arno J. Mayer, "Winston Churchill: Power Politician and Counter-Revolutionary," in Kurt H. Wolff and Barrington Moore (eds.), *The Critical Spirit: Essays in Honor of Herbert Marcuse* (Boston: Beacon Press, 1967), pp. 328-342; and Maurice Ashley, *Churchill as Historian* (New York: Charles Scribner's Sons, 1968), pp. 12-21.

instance, which claims as its foremost spokesmen Reinhold
Niebuhr (1892-1971), George Kennan (1904-   ), and Hans
Morgenthau (1904-   ), originally established its reputation
in the 1950s with a demand for recognition of the fact that
"international politics, like all politics, is a struggle for power."[32] In a manner reminiscent of the Texas congressman (and
Burke), the Realists have attacked these idealist-reform-
ers who believe in the possibility of suppressing "the chaotic
and dangerous aspirations of governments in the international field by the acceptance of some system of legal rules
and restraints."[33] The Realists have insisted that the world
would be safer if Americans (and other peoples) abandoned
universalist crusades, as well as isolationism, and agreed
that the task of every statesman is to pursue the national
interest ("defined as power") with a decent regard for others
doing the same. Of course, Morgenthau concedes, ". . . all
nations actually engaged in the struggle for power must
actually aim not at a balance—that is, equality—of power,
but at superiority of power in their own behalf." Still, if the
intelligent statesman is left alone to adjust sudden imbalances, and if the nation stands armed and ordered
behind him, stability and peace can be preserved.[34]

32. Hans Morgenthau, *Politics Among Nations* (New York: Alfred A.
Knopf, 1958), pp. 25-26. See also Morgenthau, *In Defense of the National
Interest* (New York: Alfred A. Knopf, 1951); Reinhold Niebuhr, *Chris-
tianity and Power Politics* (New York: Charles Scribner's Sons, 1940);
Niebuhr, *Man's Nature and His Communities* (New York: Charles Scrib-
ner's Sons, 1965); George F. Kennan, *American Diplomacy: 1900-1950*
(Chicago: University of Chicago Press, 1951); and Kennan, *Realities of
American Foreign Policy* (New York: W. W. Norton, 1966). For discus-
sion, see Kenneth Thompson, *Political Realism and the Crisis of World
Politics* (Princeton: Princeton University Press, 1960), pp. 3-61; James P.
Young, *The Politics of Affluence: Ideology in the United States since
World War II* (San Francisco: Chandler, 1968) pp. 145-172; and James E.
Dougherty and Robert L. Pfaltzgraff, Jr., *Contending Theories of International Relations* (Philadelphia: J. B. Lippincott, 1971), pp. 68-101. For the
perspective of another important Realist, see Anwar Hussain Syed, *Walter
Lippmann's Philosophy of International Politics* (Philadelphia: University
of Pennsylvania Press, 1963).
33. Kennan, *American Diplomacy*, p. 95.
34. The quote is from Morgenthau, *Politics among Nations*, p. 210. On

Present-day Realists have been even more pointed in their call for national unity, no crusades, and respect for the (existing, favorable) balance of power. To Henry Kissinger (1923-   ), for example, the problem is not so much American moralism abroad as it is the tendency of young people and other idealists, abetted by self-interested politicians, to assume that "the management of power" is "irrelevant, perhaps even immoral." The actual facts are quite the opposite, according to Kissinger:

All foreign policy begins with security. No great nation can afford to entrust its destiny to the whim of others. Any stable international system therefore requires a certain equilibrium of power.

Furthermore, America's own task at this point in time is clear and specific:

We cannot escape the fundamental reality that it is the United States, alone among the free nations of the world, that is capable of—and therefore responsible for—maintaining the global balance against those who would seek hegemony.

In such a situation, the principal danger we face is our domestic divisions:

We can have no higher national priority than to restore our unity. If we are mired in cynicism, recrimination, and immobility we will add to the doubts of our friends and to the temptations of our adversaries to take chances with the peace of the world.[35]

Other contemporary theorists like A. F. K. Organski

Morgenthau in particular, see Inis L. Claude, Jr., *Power and International Relations* (New York: Random House, 1962), pp. 25-37; and George Lichtheim, "The Politics of Conservative Realism," in *The Concept of Ideology and Other Essays* (New York: Vintage, 1967), pp. 129-150.

35. Henry A. Kissinger, *American Foreign Policy: Three Essays* (New York: W. W. Norton, 1969), pp. 91-97; Kissinger, Speech before the St. Louis World Affairs Council, May 12, 1975; and Kissinger, Speech at the University of Wyoming, February 4, 1976, both published by the Bureau of Public Affairs, Department of State. See also Kissinger, *Nuclear Weapons and Foreign Policy* (New York: Harper, 1957); and Kissinger, *The Necessity for Choice* (New York: Harper, 1961). For discussion, see John G. Stoessinger, *Henry Kissinger; The Anguish of Power* (New York: W. W. Norton, 1976), pp. 7-46.

(1923-) and George Liska (1922-) carry the conservative dependence on the balance of power to its logical extreme. Arguing that "the periods of balance, real or imagined, are periods of warfare, while the periods of known preponderance are periods of peace," Organski concludes that an equilibrium of power increases the danger of war by tempting both sides to believe they can win a conflict. In this view, war usually comes about because an inferior state has grown in strength to the point that a preponderance of power can no longer be brought against it. In such cases, Organski believes, war can be averted only if the once dominant state or states appease and make concessions to the newcomer.[36] Liska's position is not substantially different. Attributing the maintenance of peace since 1945 to the preponderance of American power (growing clearly "imperial" in the 1960s), Liska sees the world now moving into a more difficult era in which the United States is attempting to make "the transition from empire to leadership in [an] equilibrium. . . ." With American power no longer so readily available to maintain an "imperial order," he says, not only are relations with the Russians becoming more problematic but there is a much graver danger of violence, anarchy, and chaos in the non-Western world.[37]

One of the most brilliant and thoroughly developed versions of conservative analysis has been published by the Australian historian, Geoffrey Blainey (1930-). Devoting himself specifically to the question of what causes war, Blainey explores the history of conflict over the last three centuries in great detail. His conclusion is that, though wars

36. A. F. K. Organski, *World Politics* (New York: Alfred A. Knopf, 1958), p. 292.
37. The quote is from George Liska, *Beyond Kissinger: Ways of Conservative Statecraft* (Baltimore: Johns Hopkins University Press, 1975), p. 108. See also Liska, *Imperial America: The International Politics of Primacy* (Baltimore: Johns Hopkins University Press, 1968); and Liska, *States in Evolution* (Baltimore: Johns Hopkins University Press, 1973). For similar views, see Robert W. Tucker, *The Inequality of Nations* (New York: Basic Books, 1977).

would not occur without longstanding disputes over issues vital to the contending countries, wars do not begin until two nations disagree as to their own relative strengths. Agreement or disagreement depends on the assessment by national leaders of at least seven factors relating to their nations' war potentials:

1. Military strength and the ability to apply that strength efficiently in the likely theater of war;
2. Predictions of how outside nations will behave if war should occur;
3. Perceptions of whether there is internal unity or discord in their land and in the land of the enemy;
4. Knowledge or forgetfulness of the realities and sufferings of war;
5. Nationalism and ideology;
6. The state of the economy and also its ability to sustain the kind of war envisaged;
7. The personality and experience of those who shared in the decision.

Thus, according to Blainey, peace ultimately depends on "threats and force," that is, on the recognition of a "clear ladder of international power." For him, "any factor which increases the likelihood that nations will agree on their relative power is a potential cause of peace. One powerful cause of peace is a decisive war, for war provides the most widely accepted measure of power." As much as other conservatives, then, Blainey implies that the more we bolster the powers that be, the more peace we will enjoy.[38]

CONCLUSION

The pessimism, or fatalism, which underlies and characterizes conservative perspectives on war should now have become very obvious. Centered originally in assumptions

38. Geoffrey Blainey, *The Causes of War* (New York: Free Press, 1973), pp. 108-124, 245-249.

about human nature, this attitude has in recent years manifested itself more typically in interpretations of the nation-state and international relations. Originally offset by a belief in cosmic goodness, of late it has often been balanced by a hopeful nationalism. Yet the two conservative visions remain: that of individuals and nations as aggressive animals, i.e., as perverse and struggling organisms; and that of national groups which, because they are essentially irrational, can only be kept at peace by proper organization and management of power.

To be sure, the continued existence of pessimism in the world makes it very unlikely that conservatism, as we have defined it, will soon die out. Moreover, the maldistribution of wealth and power on the national and international scene is a standing invitation for elites to develop conservative perspectives and ideology. Yet the survival of such an ideology has been made difficult also by such historic developments as the breakdown of traditions, the growing rate of change, and the increasing uniformity and bureaucratization of society. The long-term result will probably be (and may already be) a modification of conservatism, with its spokesmen retaining emphases on community, caution, and effective leadership, but abandoning the stress on tradition and certain forms of inequality.

distribution of wealth

Meanwhile, the primary difficulty with conservative theory on war is that it is not terribly time-specific. The organismic interpretation, for example, gives almost no help (except perhaps in pointing up the relevance of energy levels) in determining why a certain conflict would have broken out at a certain time. Similarly, the order-disorder perspective tells us little about the sources of disorder or a changing balance of power. For this reason it seems clear that, in attempting to explain war, even those of solidly conservative temper and belief will have to give some attention to the interpretations advanced by representatives of the liberal and radical traditions.

CHAPTER TWO

Liberal Ideology and Theory about the Causes of War

THE LIBERAL TRADITION

While the conservative's fundamental commitment is to hierarchical community and to tradition, the liberal's is to the *individual* and to his or her *freedom and autonomy*. While the core of traditionalism is the notion that existing institutions and customs have demonstrated their worth by survival through time, the core of liberalism is the notion that individuals must be emancipated from unquestioned historic ties and ways of doing things. To the liberal, the "free" individual is the proper goal of social policy.

Still, the reader may ask, free from what? The answer to this question provides the key to understanding the historical varieties of liberalism. In the early modern era, liberalism reflected the opposition of the rising bourgeoisie to both traditional restraints (such as those of the Church), and the newly-imposed controls of centralizing monarchs (such as those of mercantilism). Later, particularly in largely bourgeois societies such as Great Britain and the United States, many liberals found their greatest threat to freedom in recently-amassed concentrations of economic wealth and power. These liberals retained the vision of a laissez-faire, free enterprise capitalism but were willing to use the state to foster and protect that capitalism.

Thus, to be "free" in the context of liberalism means to be

To be *is*frfeeble

unfettered by traditional, hierarchical authority or concen-trations of power in the state or in private hands. It means the freedom to seek private ends and it calls upon the competitive individual, with an absolute right to life, liberty, and property, to serve the common good by seeking his or her own individual gain. There is in liberalism, unlike conservative ideology, very little emphasis on the importance of belonging to a community or on the virtues of tradition. Rather, liberals and especially modern democratic liberals have repeatedly asserted the priceless *value of the individual personality*, along with the capacity of each person to control his or her destiny through the *exercise of reason.*

In contrast to conservatism, where the figure of Edmund Burke looms so large, no single theorist can serve as the fountainhead of liberal thought. Many people contributed to the development of the ideology of liberalism: John Locke in the seventeenth century; Adam Smith and Thomas Jefferson in the eighteenth century; the English utilitarians —Jeremy Bentham, James Mill, and John Stuart Mill—and the Continental liberals—François Guizot, Alexis de Tocqueville, and Joseph Mazzini—in the nineteenth century; and in the present century, Joseph Schumpeter and John Maynard Keynes. What is more, liberals themselves have different notions about their fundamental postulates.[1]

Despite such differences, it is clear that *equality* and *mobility* (both social and geographic) are more highly valued by the liberal than are the conservative tenets of hierarchy and authority. But just as the meaning of freedom

1. See Harold J. Laski, *The Rise of European Liberalism* (London: Allen and Unwin, 1936); and John H. Hallowell, *The Decline of Liberalism as an Ideology* (Berkeley: University of California Press, 1943). See also Guido de Ruggiero, *The History of European Liberalism* (Boston: Beacon Press, 1959); David Sidorsky (ed.), *The Liberal Tradition in European Thought* (New York: Capricorn Books, 1971); Louis Hartz, *The Liberal Tradition in America* (New York: Harcourt, Brace, 1955); Roger D. Masters, *The Nation Is Burdened* (New York: Alfred A. Knopf, 1967); and Arnold Wolfers and Laurence W. Martin (eds.), *The Anglo-American Tradition in Foreign Affairs* (New Haven: Yale University Press, 1956).

36   LIBERAL IDEOLOGY AND THEORY

varies in the lexicon of liberalism, so too does the meaning
of "equality." Some liberals, such as John Stuart Mill,
advocated egalitarianism while simultaneously sharing the
conservatives' concern about the "tyranny of the majority,"
and fearing that the unique talents of particular individuals
might be severely compromised in a mass society.[2] Nineteenth-century liberals opposed *complete* democracy because they believed that if all political power belonged to
"the people," then tyranny by the mass might preempt
liberty for the individual. This fear of democracy promoted
an even more intense fear of the ultimate consequences of
revolution. In fact, one behavior pattern of liberals in the
nineteenth century was to launch revolutionary movements
and, after their preliminary success, to introduce security
measures designed to restrict change to liberal (as opposed
to popular or mass democratic) ends. To repeat, then, there
is in liberalism an emphasis on "the individual" rather than
on "the people." As Irene Collins has suggested:

It is in the individual rather than in the people that the goodness
which will lead to perfection is to be found. . . . The idea of "sovereignty of the people" could not be discarded altogether, because it
was needed as a guarantee against assumptions of sovereignty by
the monarch, but henceforth sovereignty of the people was to be
recognized as limited by the liberty of the individual.[3]

Furthermore, the "equality" in liberal doctrine refers primarily to equality of opportunity and not to the equal
distribution of material and social goods to all citizens.[4]

In addition to liberalism's commitment to the autonomous individual and to the principles of equality and mobility, we have briefly noted a more complex theme in
liberalism's attitude toward the *role of the state*. The transi-

2. Among the many works of John Stuart Mill, see especially *The
Principles of Political Economy* (1848), *On Liberty* (1859), and *Representative Government* (1861).
3. Irene Collins, *Liberalism in Nineteenth-Century Europe* (London:
Historical Association, 1957), p. 9.
4. See Richard Lichtman, "The Facade of Equality in Liberal Democratic Theory," *Socialist Revolution*, 1 (January-February 1970), p. 87.

tion from the early phase of liberalism to its later phase did not occur easily or simultaneously in Western nations. Nineteenth-century liberals in Great Britain, for example, were as one with conservatives in advocating the doctrine of the minimal state. The British liberal demanded freedom for the individual from the constraints of the state because, as British political scientist Maurice Cranston suggests, he has regarded "the state as an instrument of value only in so far as it could serve the interests of the individual person."[5] At the same time, recognizing that the principle of liberty in its extreme form can lead to anarchy, the British liberal assigned the state certain specific responsibilities, such as civil order, defense against foreign intrusion, and the security of private property.

Complementing the liberal dedication to the minimal state, particularly in Britain, was the economic doctrine known as "laissez-faire." Liberals such as Adam Smith, David Ricardo, and John Stuart Mill argued that a nation's economy had its own natural laws of operation and that state interference in the economy could only be damaging in the long run. The "free market" existed prior to the state and was therefore more "natural." On these grounds, nineteenth-century liberals continued their longstanding fight against the restrictive mercantilist policies of the seventeenth and eighteenth centuries in favor of freedom of trade without the constraints of the state. Laissez-faire economics was therefore an important corollary of the liberal doctrine of the minimal state.

In contrast, Continental liberals (such as the *étatiste* liberals in France and the German liberals who developed the concept of the *Rechtsstaat*) ultimately renounced the "British" doctrine of the minimal state. Even more than in Great Britain and the United States, they had been subjected in the late nineteenth century to a continuous and devastating attack by their conservative and radical opponents for

5. Maurice Cranston, *Freedom* (New York: Basic Books, 1967), p. 50.

excluding new social classes from the privileges enjoyed by liberals and for failing to strengthen the nation by assisting rapid industrialization. The response of these liberals was to move toward identifying freedom with self-government and toward pressing for an enlarged democratic state.

The Continental liberals thus led the way to that more positive view of the role of the state that eventually came to prevail in liberal doctrine. By the early twentieth century, liberals in virtually every Western nation had followed the Continental pattern by embarking on active programs of state intervention in economic and social matters. These "new" liberals attempted to use the state as an agency of social reform, ostensibly to ensure that power would be widely shared among groups representing different segments of society. Inherent in this liberal program of the "welfare state" is an older, "pluralistic" conception of the government as a neutral force, independent and serving equally the claims of all organized groups. Such pluralist notions draw upon themes in liberal thought that go back at least as far as the arguments espoused by James Madison in *The Federalist* (Number 10). According to these pluralist assumptions, the primary locus of power lies in the *political* system and not (as radicals assert) in the economic system.[6]

Meanwhile, throughout the twentieth century, "old" liberals have continued to look upon the state as the primary

6. Among the leading pluralist analyses of the political power structure, see Robert Dahl, *Who Governs?* (New Haven: Yale University Press, 1961) and, by the same author, *Modern Political Analysis* (Englewood Cliffs, N.J.: Prentice-Hall, 1963) and *Pluralist Democracy in the United States* (Chicago: Rand McNally, 1967). See also Arnold M. Rose, *The Power Structure: Political Process in American Society* (New York: Oxford University Press, 1967). For criticisms of pluralist theory, see, among others, Michael Paul Rogin, *The Intellectuals and McCarthy: The Radical Specter* (Cambridge: MIT Press, 1967); Ralph Miliband, *The State in Capitalist Society* (New York: Basic Books, 1969); Theodore J. Lowi, *The End of Liberalism: Ideology, Policy, and the Crisis of Public Authority* (New York: W. W. Norton, 1969); and Milton Mankoff, "Power in Advanced Capitalist Society: A Review Essay on Recent Elitist and Marxist Criticism of Pluralist Theory," *Social Problems*, 17 (Winter 1970), pp. 418-430.

threat to individual liberty and to play down the dangers inherent in a free-enterprise system increasingly dominated by concentrations of private wealth. Often in close alliance with conservatives (or, as in the United States, calling themselves conservatives), such liberals fought the trend toward the welfare-statism of the more active liberals. Yet such disagreements could not obscure the fact that they shared with the activists a primary emphasis on the importance of the individual's freedom of action.

Thus, while liberalism is certainly an ambiguous and complex ideology, among its variations it is possible to discern several continuing tenets: the view of *human beings as potentially rational and self-reliant*; the desire to *free them to exercise their capacities*; the stress on *equality and social mobility*; *opposition to all forms of power that might impair or oppose the achievement of these social ends*; and, finally, the firmly held belief that the ideals of *freedom and democracy are most fully realized in capitalist societies.*

LIBERAL THEORY ABOUT THE CAUSES OF WAR

As was the case with conservative theory, our purpose in this section is to examine how liberals have explained the coming of war and to determine the extent to which the ideology of liberalism has influenced the construction of such theory.

As we have suggested, liberalism is committed emphatically to the freedom of the individual and sees the individual as capable and needful of exercising inherent rights to life, liberty, and property. From the perspective of the liberal it follows that wherever a state limits its citizens' freedom, there is potential for conflict and violence both within the state and in its foreign relations (since autocracy inevitably distorts public understanding, stymies normal cooperation, and tempts its rulers to reduce popular dissatisfaction through distraction). The most obvious implication of this perspective for liberal theory is that the risk of war would be

greatly reduced if the world were composed entirely of liberal nation-states interacting openly and pursuing free trade.

One of the earliest and most eloquent proponents of such a view was the eighteenth-century Germany philosopher of the Enlightenment, Immanuel Kant (1724-1804). Rejecting the pessimism of many of his conservative contemporaries, who believed that war could never be completely eliminated, Kant in one of his last works (*Eternal Peace*, 1795) made a fervent plea for universal peace, and a prediction regarding its accomplishment, through a voluntary world federation of republics:

> By the expenditure of all the resources of the commonwealth in military preparations against each other, by the devastations occasioned by war, and still more by the necessity of holding themselves continually in readiness for it, the full development of the capacities of mankind are undoubtedly retarded in their progress; but, on the other hand, the very evils which thus arise, compel men to find out means against them. A law of equilibrium is thus discovered for the regulation of the really wholesome antagonisms of contiguous States as it springs up out of their freedom; and a united power, giving emphasis to this law, is constituted, whereby there is introduced a universal condition of public security among the nations.[7]

 According to Kant, the strength of any nation-state derived from the amount of liberty enjoyed by its subjects. In order to survive in the competition among nation-states, therefore, rulers would be forced to grant greater liberty to their subjects until, finally, the republican form of government would become a pattern for the entire world. At that point, as a result of the internal perfection of these republics, it ought to be possible for them to act on maxims that could be universalized without conflict.

The fact is, however, that the international system (in

7. See Kant's "The Principle of Progress" in *Eternal Peace and Other International Essays*, translated by W. Hastie (Boston: The World Peace Foundation, 1914), p. 17, and the discussion in Kenneth N. Waltz, "Kant, Liberalism, and War," *American Political Science Review*, 56 (June 1962), p. 336.

Kant's time and now) includes a variety of "authoritarian" regimes deemed by liberals to be necessarily more warlike than those limited governments that respect the rights of their citizens. Indeed, liberal states of the contemporary "Free World" see themselves as living under substantial threat of external aggression. A common liberal explanation of war, then, stresses the existence of despotic or totalitarian nation-states hostile to the political and economic interests of liberal democracies. This liberal viewpoint is well illustrated by the attitudes of Woodrow Wilson, who believed strongly that national self-determination and self-government under law were essential preconditions of international peace. (For more on Wilson, see Chapter 4.)

This is not to say, however, that war cannot occur between liberal nations or that a liberal nation will never aggress against a more authoritarian one (as the United States did against Mexico in 1846, for example). Though liberals believe that human beings are potentially rational, they also acknowledge that certain situations can cause persons or groups to misperceive objective reality and develop images or stereotypes that are independent of actual experience. Moreover, liberals contend, individuals can experience personal frustrations that will ultimately lead to aggressive behavior.[8] Furthermore, there are times, even with liberal democracies, when certain groups which are more sympathetic to war than others acquire inordinate power. Finally, there is the possibility that a pluralistic or balanced sharing of power among nation-states becomes difficult to maintain, and war then becomes highly probable.

Thus the liberal, when not attributing war to an outside force, tends to see it as resulting either from psychological factors or from temporary imbalances that serve to create instability within the domestic or international systems. According to many liberal theorists, the eventual decision

8. See Joseph Frankel, *Contemporary International Theory and the Behavior of States* (New York and London: Oxford University Press, 1973), pp. 65-66.

for war is based on a "crisis mentality" among members of the leading groups. Or, using the jargon of the social sciences, some liberals argue that in order to understand the coming of war we must engage in "situational analysis [which] assumes that the action of an agent (in this case an international actor) is a function of the immediate situation it confronts." In short, the main emphasis in much liberal theory is on the psychological confusion or stress experiences of decision-makers and on fear generated *during the crisis itself*.[9]

In more specific theoretical terms, liberal scholars have generally relied on one (or more) of three basic theories: "social-psychological," "structural-functionalist," or "group conflict." These theories, particularly the social-psychological and the structural-functionalist, differ more in emphasis than in kind. For example, social-psychological theorists view both domestic and international conflict almost solely as a consequence of psychological discontent or malfunction. Structural-functionalists, on the other hand, generally explain such phenomena without explicit reference to psychological factors. They also warn against a psychological reductionism that does not distinguish between violence carried out by abnormal, pathological individuals and violence that results from the personal tensions and frustrations of people living in a "disequilibrated" social system.[10]

9. See Charles F. Hermann, "International Crisis as a Situational Variable," in James N. Rosenau (ed.), *International Politics and Foreign Policy* (New York: Free Press, 1969), p. 409; L. L. Farrar, Jr., "The Limits of Choice: July 1914 Reconsidered," *Journal of Conflict Resolution*, 16 (March 1972), pp. 4-5; Barton J. Bernstein, "'Great Crises Produce Great Men': A Review Essay on Henry Fairlie's *The Kennedy Promise*," *Peace and Change*, 1 (Spring 1973), pp. 74-78; and Alastair Buchan, *War in Modern Society* (London: C. A. Watts, 1966), pp. 20-23. See also Charles F. Hermann (ed.), *International Crises: Insights from Behavioral Research* (New York: Free Press, 1972).

10. See, for example, Chalmers Johnson, *Revolutionary Change* (Boston: Little, Brown, 1966), pp. 13, 56-57. As Johnson points out: "Just as an individual personality cannot be derived entirely from the social system in which it is formed, the social system and its needs and processes cannot be derived entirely from a study of the personalities that exist within it." See

Nevertheless, as we shall see, both approaches derive from very similar assumptions, foremost of which is that "equilibrium" is far more desirable than unpredictable, uncertain structural change.

Group conflict theorists are not only unimpressed by purely psychological explanations of conflict but also reject the structural-functionalist view that society is a system held in equilibrium by the mutually accommodating interaction of its constitutent parts. From this perspective, society (and the international order) is inherently divided and competitive because of the continuous struggle among groups (and nation-states) for limited resources. Such theorists are thus more likely to acknowledge coercive relationships and the domination of some groups (or nation-states) over others. For them, then, social integration is to a great extent a function of coercion or balance of power.

Despite the acknowledged differences among these theories, the ideological assumptions undergirding all three remain essentially liberal. All presuppose, for example, considerable faith in the ability of human reason to cope with continuing difficulties; none suggests that war is an inherent characteristic either of human nature (as many conservatives would assert) or of capitalism (the radical view). Hopefully such underlying assumptions will become more apparent as we describe the basic premises of each of the three theories and then discuss the ways they have been used by liberal historians of World War I and World War II (see Chapters 4 and 5).

war is not natural

Social-Psychological Theory

Given their ideological commitment to the importance of the individual, a substantial number of liberal theorists understandably have been strongly influenced by the find-

also Anthony D. Smith, *The Concept of Social Change: A Critique of the Functionalist Theory of Social Change* (London and Boston: Routledge and Kegan Paul, 1973), pp. 122-125.

ings of psychologists and social-psychologists. In attempting to determine why persons behave aggressively—in both domestic and international contexts—they have focused almost exclusively on those elements of experience that cause extreme discontent among individuals and that lead, eventually, to "irrational" behavior. In the process, largely as a consequence of their general optimism regarding the actual or potential benefits of the prevailing economic and social systems, they have tended to denigrate the influence of economic and social factors in causing war, stressing instead the importance of such "state-of-mind" concepts as tensions and anxieties, frustrated expectations, and relative deprivation. In this respect, these liberal theorists have followed the direction of Alexis de Tocqueville in his classic study of the French Revolution, concluding that social conflict is likely to occur in periods of improving economic and social conditions (i.e., as a result of a "revolution of rising expectations").

Frustration causes Revolutions

A good example of this theoretical orientation is Ted Robert Gurr's *Why Men Rebel* (1970). Here Gurr (1936-   ) advances the broad-ranging theory of relative deprivation, which is the discrepancy between what individuals expect and what they in fact obtain. He hypothesizes that as individual dissatisfaction deriving from this discrepancy becomes widespread, the greater will be the probability and intensity of mass action, violence, or revolution. To state the proposition another way, frustration rises as expectations exceed supply. In such instances, individuals are likely to experience anger and hostility. These feelings intensify and become focused on public officials or prominent decision-makers, in which case the frustrated and angry individuals are motivated to act aggressively—even violently—toward these leaders. Unfulfilled expectations are not limited to economic matters but may also involve considerations of power, political participation, and declining status or prestige. The increasing and widespread dissatisfaction imposes upon the ruling elites a requirement of "tension-management," since new ways must be found to satisfy public demands if society is to maintain itself in relative equilibrium. In terms of the theory of relative deprivation, then, group conflict, revolution, and war are all viewed essentially as results of displaced psychological discontent.[11]

Gurr's theory draws heavily from studies by contemporary psychologists and social-psychologists, such as John Dollard and Leonard W. Doob, regarding the so-called frustration-aggression hypothesis. This hypothesis suggests that frustration (defined as experiencing interference in achieving a particular goal) frequently produces aggressive behavior. When a personal goal is thwarted, the individual is often compelled to vent his or her anger by attacking the agent of that frustration or an available substitute. In elaborating on this hypothesis (which, to the extent that an enraged individual behaves "rationally," is obviously as relevant to radical as to liberal theory), Gurr begins by locating the source of discontent in the individual, and then generalizes this process to the group level.[12]

11. See Ted Robert Gurr, *Why Men Rebel* (Princeton: Princeton University Press, 1970); and Perez Zagorin, "Theories of Revolution in Contemporary Historiography," *Political Science Quarterly*, 88 (March 1973), pp. 43-44. A detailed critique of *Why Men Rebel* is offered by Joseph M. Firestone in "Continuities in the Theory of Violence," *Journal of Conflict Resolution*, 18 (March 1974), pp. 117-141. See also James C. Davies, "Toward a Theory of Revolution," *American Sociological Review*, 27 (February 1962), pp. 6, 8; and Isaac Kramnick, "Reflections on Revolution: Definition and Explanation in Recent Scholarship," *History and Theory*, 11 (1972), pp. 41-45. For a more general treatment of social-psychological theory, see Hans Toch, *Social Psychology and Social Movements* (Indianapolis and New York: Bobbs-Merrill, 1965).

12. For an excellent discussion of the frustration-aggression hypothesis, its strengths and weaknesses, and its leading theorists, see James E. Dougherty and Robert L. Pfaltzgraff, *Contending Theories of International Relations* (Philadelphia: J. B. Lippincott, 1971), pp. 212-221. As these authors point out (p. 218), "The frustration-aggression school has attempted to move from the individual to the social level more by logical inference than by experimentation." Also see John Dollard, Leonard W. Doob, Neal E. Miller, O. H. Mowrer, and Robert R. Sears, *Frustration and Aggression* (New Haven: Yale University Press, 1939); Leonard Berkowitz, *Aggression: A Social Psychological Analysis* (New York: McGraw-Hill, 1962); Berkowitz, "The Frustration-Aggression Hypothesis Revisited,"

A closely related liberal interpretation of the factors that impel individuals toward collective action is that of "status anxiety." Thus, while acknowledging the crucial role of economic factors in explaining group conflict during conditions of depression (as in the United States from 1893 to 1897), many liberal scholars assert that psychological concerns or frustrations over "status" are also important, and that they become of paramount significance in understanding similar activism during periods of prosperity (as in the United States during 1900-1917).

Such social-psychological explanations for group behavior were used by Richard Hofstadter (1916-1973) in his provocative studies of the Populist and Progressive eras, as well as in his analysis of recent "pseudo-conservatism" in the United States.[13] In his highly influential book, *The Age of Reform* (1955), Hofstadter characterized the Populists as mildly irrational precursors of the McCarthyism of the 1950s and also proposed the thesis that individuals became involved in the Progressive movement of the early twentieth century "not because of economic deprivations but primarily because they were victims of an upheaval in status that took place in the United States during the closing decades of the nineteenth century and the early years of the twentieth century." According to him, leaders of Progressivism were motivated to act politically because of "the changed pattern in the distribution of deference and pow-

---

in Berkowitz (ed.), *Roots of Aggression: A Re-Examination of the Frustration-Aggression Hypothesis* (New York: Atherton, 1969), Chap. 2; and Ted Robert Gurr, "The Revolution-Social Change Nexus: Some Old Theories and New Hypotheses," *Comparative Politics*, 5 (April 1973), pp. 364-368.

13. See particularly Hofstadter's *The Age of Reform* (New York: Vintage, 1955); *Anti-Intellectualism in American Life* (New York: Alfred A. Knopf, 1963); *The Paranoid Style in American Politics* (New York: Vintage, 1967); and "The Pseudo-Conservative Revolt," in Daniel Bell (ed.), *The New American Right* (New York: Criterion Books, 1955). Hofstadter modified certain of his views in *The Progressive Historians: Turner, Beard, Parrington* (New York: Alfred A. Knopf, 1969); see especially pp. 456-466.

er."[14] He was therefore concerned not so much with the external conditions of American society in that period as with the "inward social and psychological position" of Progressives themselves.[15]

Precisely the same kind of analysis informs Hofstadter's explanation of the Spanish-American War at the end of the nineteenth century and the acquisition of the Philippine Islands after that war. Rejecting the importance of imperialist ambition and stressing instead the role of popular humanitarianism and jingoism, Hofstadter argued: "The Philippine crisis is inseparable from the war crisis, and the war crisis itself is inseparable from the larger constellation that might be called 'the psychic crisis of the 1890s.'" Internal frustrations engendered by economic depression and domes-

14. Hofstadter, *The Age of Reform*, p. 135. "The central idea of the status politics conception," according to Daniel Bell, a prominent liberal sociologist, "is that groups that are advancing in wealth and social position are often as anxious and politically feverish as groups that have become déclassé." See *The End of Ideology* (New York: Collier Books, 1961), pp. 111, 117-118.

15. Hofstadter, *The Age of Reform*, p. 135. This interpretation has been severely criticized by numerous scholars. One pertinent criticism is that the status-anxiety hypothesis is not validated by empirical evidence at the state level, where it fails to explain the differences between middle-class Progressives and their contemporary conservative opponents. Furthermore, on a broader level, it has been argued that the attempt to explain collective behavior by relying primarily on psychological factors has often resulted in an overemphasis on nonrational motivations or even on pathological characteristics of participants in such movements. This approach, therefore, tends to obscure the situational conditions and legitimate economic and social grievances out of which reform movements and social conflict arise. Of the many critical assessments of the status-anxiety thesis, see particularly Richard B. Sherman, "The Status-Revolution and Massachusetts Progressive Leadership," *Political Science Quarterly*, 78 (March 1963); Robert W. Doherty, "Status-Anxiety and American Reform: Some Alternatives," *American Quarterly*, 19 (Summer 1967); David P. Thelen, "Social Tensions and the Origins of Progressivism," *Journal of American History*, 56 (September 1969); and Peter G. Filene, "An Obituary for 'The Progressive Movement,'" *American Quarterly*, 22 (Spring 1970). For a harsh critique of the status-anxiety thesis as employed by Seymour Martin Lipset and Earl Raab to explain "extremism" in their recent work, *The Politics of Unreason* (New York: Harper and Row, 1971), see Leo P. Ribuffo, "'Pluralism' and American History," *Dissent* (June 1971), pp. 272-278.

tic unrest stimulated an irrational urge for external aggression. In the concluding paragraphs of his essay Hofstadter clearly reveals his indebtedness to social-psychological theory: "Men often respond to frustration with acts of aggression, and allay their anxieties by threatening acts against others. It is revealing that the underdog forces in American society showed a considerably higher responsiveness to the idea of war with Spain than the groups that were satisfied with their economic or political positions."[16]

Though psychology and social-psychology have long been established disciplines, it was only in the years immediately preceding and during World War II that social scientists, among them Harold Lasswell (1902-   ) and Hadley Cantril (1906-   ), began studying the causes of war from such perspectives. Finding the frustration-aggression hypothesis a useful tool for understanding international conflict, they developed an analogy between war and interpersonal violence. Nations as well as individuals, they said, must have expressive outlets for pent-up frustrations. As Lasswell described it, "Wars and revolutions are avenues of discharge for collective insecurity and stand in competition with every alternative means of dissipating mass tension."[17] In the opinion of these scholars and their successors, the causes of war are not to be found in rational considerations such as the need for new markets or to defend national territory. Neither are they to be located in the instinctual drives of human beings, as conservatives assert. Rather, the roots of conflict lie in inner tensions, culturally conditioned anxieties, and the resulting distortions of perceptions.[18]

16. Hofstadter, "Cuba, the Philippines, and Manifest Destiny," reprinted in revised form in *The Paranoid Style in American Politics,* pp. 145-187.

17. Harold Lasswell, *World Politics and Personal Insecurity* (New York: McGraw-Hill, 1935), p. 25.

18. See Haldey Cantril (ed.), *Tensions That Cause Wars* (Urbana: University of Illinois Press, 1950); Caroline Playne, *The Neuroses of the Nations* (London: Allen and Unwin, 1925); E. F. M. Durbin and John Bowlby, *Personal Aggressiveness and War* (New York: Columbia University Press, 1939); Mark A. May, *A Social Psychology of War and Peace*

Stoessinger fits here!

Many students of war causation in the 1950s and 1960s, like Cantril, Kenneth Boulding, and Leon Festinger, placed great emphasis on the significance of such factors as "images," "stereotypes," and "cognitive dissonance." Viewing these phenomena as crucially important to the policy-maker (and citizen) during "normal" times, they saw them as even more significant when a "crisis" situation developed and emotions became intensified. Their claim that such factors cause wars involved at least two basic assumptions: (1) if more people were "rational" there would be better perception and less misunderstanding, and (2) cooperation is the "natural" condition of the international system and only when there are nonsystemic (i.e., psychological) influences involved do wars occur.[19]

It should be noted that in the late 1960s and the 1970s there emerged a modified version of social-psychological theory as applied to international affairs. This approach, as used by Robert Abelson, Robert Axelrod, Robert Jervis, and John Steinbrunner, among others, places greater stress on cognitive (as opposed to affective and emotional) factors, and it views with some skepticism the characteristic optimism of liberals regarding the "natural" inclination for cooperation among nation-states.[20] As Robert Abelson

(New Haven: Yale University Press, 1943); T. H. Pear (ed.), *Psychological Factors of Peace and War* (New York: Philosophical Library, 1950); Otto Klineberg, *Tensions Affecting International Understanding* (New York: Social Science Research Council, 1950); and Alix Strachey, *The Unconscious Motives of War* (New York: International Universities Press, 1957). For a general discussion see Kenneth N. Waltz, *Man, the State, and War* (New York: Columbia University Press, 1959), pp. 42-79.

19. Kenneth Boulding, *The Image* (Ann Arbor, Mich.: University of Michigan Press, 1956); Boulding, "National Images and International Systems," *Journal of Conflict Resolution*, 3 (June 1959), pp. 120-131; and Leon Festinger, *Conflict, Decision and Dissonance* (Stanford, Calif.: Stanford University Press, 1964).

20. Robert Ableson *et al.* (eds.), *Theories of Cognitive Consistency* (Chicago: Rand McNally, 1968); Robert Axelrod, *Conflict of Interest: A Theory of Divergent Goals with Application to Politics* (Chicago: Markham, 1970); Axelrod (ed.), *Structure of Decision: The Cognitive Maps of*

50   LIBERAL IDEOLOGY AND THEORY

suggests, "There are plenty of 'cold' cognitive factors which produce inaccurate world-views."[21] These scholars argue, therefore, that more attention must be paid to the problem of how even perfectly unemotional and rational people draw inferences from highly ambiguous evidence. For, as Jervis points out, "some important causes of misperception are traceable to general cognitive processes rather than to an individual's disturbed psyche." Furthermore, these theorists believe that the importance of "conflict of interest" in international relations has been ignored by most social-psychological studies. "More specifically," writes Jervis, pointing to the need for supra-individual studies, "there is little comprehension of the consequences of the lack of a sovereign in the international realm and little analysis of the reasons why even highly rational decision-makers often conclude that they must be extremely suspicious and mistrustful."[22]

Social-psychological theorists of international relations thus concentrate attention on a variety of motivational and perceptual factors that, in their opinion, lead nation-states toward war. For several reasons, this theoretical approach is highly compatible with the liberal tenets discussed earlier. For example, it relies for much of its explanatory power on the emotional and cognitive stress experienced by individual

Political Elites (Princeton: Princeton University Press, 1976); Robert Jervis, *The Logic of Images in International Relations* (Princeton: Princeton University Press, 1970); Jervis, *Perception and Misperception in International Politics* (Princeton: Princeton University Press, 1976); John Steinbrunner, *Some Effects of Decision Procedures on Policy Outcomes* (Cambridge, Mass.: M.I.T. Center for International Studies, 1970); and Steinbrunner, *The Cybernetic Theory of Decision* (Princeton: Princeton University Press, 1974). See also Ross Stagner, *Psychological Aspects of International Conflict* (Belmont, Calif.: Cole, 1967); and Ralph K. White, *Nobody Wanted War: Misperception in Vietnam and Other Wars* (New York: Anchor Books, 1970).

21. Abelson, "The Structure of Belief Systems," in Roger Schank and Kenneth Colby (eds.), *Computer Models of Thought and Language* (San Francisco: W. H. Freeman, 1973), p. 288.

22. Jervis, *Perception and Misperception in International Politics*, pp. 4, 8.

decision-makers during a crisis. It also provides a way in which hostility originating in individual frustrations and misperceptions can be translated into conflict among nation-states. Furthermore, it plays down long-range, structural factors, such as the imperatives of a particular economic system. The major "lens" of the theory is invariably directed at the potentially rational individual who, for a variety of identifiable reasons, has behaved (either individually or collectively) in a nonrational manner or has formulated an inaccurate world-view.

Other social scientists writing from liberal assumptions acknowledge the significance of psychological factors but view them as only very partial explanations. These scholars, who are brought together in the following sections under the theory categories of "structural-functionalism" and "group conflict," argue that in order to explain domestic and international conflict it is always necessary to return to the level of political analysis. Both groups may be distinguished from the social-psychologists, among other ways, by their greater insistence on comprehending the total social system.

Structural-Functionalist Theory

Structural-functionalism is a second approach frequently employed by liberal scholars to comprehend social reality.[23] The original concepts in this case are strikingly similar to those of social-psychology. In both instances, synthesis proceeds from a virtually identical theoretical basis: the

---

23. There are those who would argue for important distinctions within structural-functionalism itself. These distinctions exist primarily between the "structuralists," who simply wish to describe individual institutions in detail, and the "functionalists," who are concerned with examining institutions only as they contribute to the whole. For an excellent account of the heterogeneity within structural-functionalism, see N. J. Demerath, "Synecdoche and Structural-Functionalism," in N. J. Demerath and Richard A. Peterson (eds.), *System, Change and Conflict* (New York: Free Press, 1967), pp. 502-506. For purposes of this book we view structural-functionalism as a theoretical unity that can be described and evaluated in its entirety.

"tension-need" theory of behavior.[24] According to this theory (of which the "frustration-aggression" hypothesis is an obvious variety), individuals, being otherwise sound, experience tension when their needs are not met (for example, when there is lack of affection) and will behave so as to reduce that tension. From this perspective, the personality of the individual is most ideal when it approximates a state of "psychic homeostasis," or a relative absence of unmet needs. Reducing instability to a state of homeostasis thus becomes an important social goal, achieved either by reducing needs or by altering the expectations of individuals.

This tension-need concept has been incorporated into the major works of Talcott Parsons (1902-   ), the preeminent theorist of structural-functionalism. In his earlier writings, Parsons focused on those psychological needs and values that in his view motivated human behavior. In *The Social System* (1951), for example, the basic problem addressed by Parsons was to explain the adjustment of individuals or social groups to one another. In responding to this problem, his debt to the tension-need theory of behavior is clearly evident:

> We may say that the need for *security* in the motivational sense is the need to preserve stable cathexis of social objects, including collectivities. Tendencies to dominance or submission, aggressiveness or compulsive dependence, then, may be interpreted as manifestations of insecurity. The need for a feeling of adequacy on the other hand, we may say, is the need to feel able to live up to the normative standards of the expectation system, to conform in that sense.[25]

In his later writings in the 1950s and 1960s, Parsons augmented his analysis of individual motivation and began to concentrate on the *entire society* as a self-maintaining, homeostatic *system*. Indeed, the concepts of "system" and

24. For an elaboration see Wayne Hield, "The Study of Change in Social Science," *The British Journal of Sociology*, 5 (March 1964), pp. 1-11.

25. Talcott Parsons, *The Social System* (Glencoe, Ill.: Free Press, 1951), p. 261.

"system analysis" are central to an understanding of structural-functionalism as a sociological theory. In moving from
a concentration on individuals to a concern with the functioning of the total social system, Parsons serves as a
bridge between social-psychological and structural-functionalist theories.[26]

Structural-functional analysis views the social system as
being composed of interdependent and mutually accommodating structures, that is, structures that fit "naturally" with
each other. It is therefore essentially a theory of consensus.

[margin note: a theory of consensus]

26. As Parsons once wrote: "The most essential condition of successful
dynamic analysis is continual and systematic reference of every problem to
the state of the system as a whole." See *Essays in Sociological Theory*
(Glencoe, Ill.: Free Press, 1949), p. 21. Other major works by Parsons, in
addition to those already cited, include: *The Structure of Social Action*
(New York: McGraw-Hill, 1937); *Structure and Process in Modern Societies* (New York: Free Press, 1960); *Society: Evolutionary and Comparative Perspectives* (Englewood Cliffs, N.J.: Prentice-Hall, 1966); *Sociological Theory and Modern Society* (New York: Free Press, 1967); *The System
of Modern Societies* (Englewood Cliffs, N.J.: Prentice-Hall, 1971).
    Favorable discussions of Parsons' ideas may be found in Robert A.
Nisbet's *Social Change and History* (New York: Oxford University Press,
1969), pp. 228-239, 256-267; and Harold J. Bershady, *Ideology and Social
Knowledge* (New York: Oxford University Press, 1972), *passim*. Three
harshly critical reviews of Parsons are Tom Bottomore, "Out of This
World," *New York Review of Books* (Nov. 6, 1969), pp. 34-39; Harold
Jacobs, "Aspects of the Political Sociology of Talcott Parsons," *Berkeley
Journal of Sociology*, 14 (1969), pp. 58-72; and particularly Alvin W.
Gouldner, *The Coming Crisis of Western Sociology* (New York: Basic
Books, 1970), pp. 167-338. Also see Max Black (ed.), *The Social Theories
of Talcott Parsons: A Critical Examination* (Englewood Cliffs, N.J.:
Prentice-Hall, 1961).
    Other important examples of structural-functionalism are: Wilbert E.
Moore, *Industrial Relations and the Social Order*, rev. ed. (New York:
Macmillan, 1951); Moore, *Social Change* (Englewood Cliffs, N.J.: Pren-
tice-Hall, 1963); Marion J. Levy, Jr., *The Structure of Society* (Princeton:
Princeton University Press, 1952); Robert K. Merton, *Social Theory and
Social Structure*, rev. ed. (Glencoe, Ill.: Free Press, 1964); Merton, *On
Theoretical Sociology* (New York: Free Press, 1967); Neil Smelser and
Talcott Parsons, *Economy and Society* (Glencoe, Ill.: Free Press, 1957);
Smelser, *Theory of Collective Behavior* (New York: Free Press, 1962); and
Chalmers Johnson, *Revolutionary Change*. For an examination of the
impact of structural-functionalism on the writing of history, see Louis
Galambos, "Parsonian Sociology and Post-Progressive History," *Social
Science Quarterly*, 50 (June 1969), pp. 24-45.

stability, and equilibrium. It is also a theory of change—both *within* a social system and *of* a social system. To be sure, as its critics maintain, there is a bias in favor of order and stability inherent in the concepts of structural-functionalism. But to determine what functions must be performed in order for a system to maintain equilibrium is quite different from arguing that these requisite functions will always *be* performed. This is the point made by Robert Merton (1910-   ), another major structural-functionalist, who, while acknowledging that functionalist analysis is usually directed toward "the statics of social structure," notes that it also deals with "the dynamics of social change." Merton suggests that the dysfunctional elements inherent in all social systems serve as change agents directly affecting the structures of those systems.[27]

Other structural-functionalists have been even more precise in defining universal and persistent sources of change in social systems. Wilbert Moore, for example, discovers the recurrent origins of change in the lack of correspondence between the individual's ideals and the reality he or she encounters.[28] Another leading functionalist, anthropologist Raymond Firth, reaches a similar conclusion: "The essence of the dynamic process lies in the continuous operation of the individual psyche, with its potential of unsatisfied desires—for more security, more knowledge, more status, more power, more approval."[29] We can observe, therefore, the importance for both social-psychologists and many structural-functionalists of such "state-of-mind" theories as relative deprivation, frustration-aggression, tension-need, status-anxiety, and cognitive distortion leading to misperceptions and false images.

Important elaborations of Parsonian structural-functionalism are provided by Neil Smelser's *Theory of Collective*

27. Robert Merton, *Social Theory and Social Structure*, p. 40.
28. Wilbert Moore, *Social Change*, p. 18.
29. Raymond Firth, *Elements of Social Organization* (Boston: Beacon Press, 1963), p. 86.

Behavior (1962) and Chalmers Johnson's *Revolutionary Change* (1966). Here the common theoretical goal is to identify those factors that promote or inhibit violent group conflict. Smelser's and Johnson's categories are perhaps the most systematic yet developed for this purpose. Surprisingly, however, they do not employ their theories to explain the causes of war, despite the fact that war, like revolution, "is inseparable from the social context in which it occurs."[30] For examples of how structural-functionalist theory may be used to comprehend conflict among nation-states, we must turn to studies specifically in the area of international politics and foreign policy.

Here again, Talcott Parsons establishes the framework for discussion when he writes of "the ways in which modern societies constitute a single system."[31] Indeed, one of the most significant recent trends in the study of international relations is to regard the world as a developing *international system*. We have seen how social-psychological theorists attempt to stretch their frustration-aggression hypothesis so as to cover not only individuals and groups, but also nation-states. In similar fashion, structural-functionalists such as George Modelski, Herbert J. Spiro, and others have begun to translate their notions of equilibrium and stability within individuals or a particular social system in such a way as to encompass the totality of social systems.[32]

30. On the theories of Smelser and Johnson, see Robert F. Berkhofer, Jr., *A Behavioral Approach to Historical Analysis* (New York: Free Press, 1969), pp. 303-313; Alvin Gouldner, *The Coming Crisis of Western Sociology*, pp. 368-370; Richard P. Applebaum, *Theories of Social Change* (Chicago: Markham, 1970); Ted Robert Gurr, "The Revolution-Social Change Nexus," pp. 368-371; Perez Zagorin, "Theories of Revolution in Contemporary Historiography," pp. 51-52; and Isaac Kramnick, "Reflections on Revolution," pp. 48-53.

31. Parsons, *The System of Modern Societies*, p. 139.

32. Major treatments include George Modelski, *The Communist International System* (Princeton: Princeton University Press, 1960); and Herbert J. Spiro, *World Politics: The Global System* (Homewood, Ill.: Dorsey, 1966). Other "systems theorists" (e.g., Morton A. Kaplan) and "integration, or community theorists" (e.g., Ernst Haas, Amitai Etzioni), though critical of the "self-equilibriating tendencies" in Parson's arrangements,

One of the underlying principles of this kind of "systems perspective" is "reciprocity": a system possesses interdependent parts engaged in mutual (or reciprocally functional) interchanges. Thus, the international system closely resembles other social systems in that its existence requires the performance of certain functions (e.g., foreign trade, the exchange of information). Furthermore, it has a structure (or a pattern of operation) and is composed of identifiable, interdependent parts that are functionally related to each other. Nation-states are obviously the most important component of this international system, but there are others, such as the United Nations, the Roman Catholic Church, and multinational corporations. These components, in turn, are influenced by environmental factors (such as famines, population trends, the need for raw materials, the development of technologies) that condition their behavior.

From this perspective, then, a structural-functionalist would typically argue that conflict is characteristic of social systems with insufficient internal organization or "integration," and that wars occur because the world community of nations is not yet a maturely functioning, homeostatic unit in equilibrium. Structural-functionalists would like to find at the level of the international system the same patterns of interaction that operate domestically.[33] As it happens, however, the frequency of war, defined as a breakdown in the

---

have obviously been greatly influenced by the latter's theories. Overall descriptions and assessments are provided by Charles A. McClelland, "Systems Theory and Human Conflict," in Elton B. McNeil (ed.), *The Nature of Human Conflict* (Englewood Cliffs, N.J.: Prentice-Hall, 1965), pp. 250-273; Dougherty and Pfaltzgraff, *Contending Theories of International Relations*, pp. 102-137; Paul Taylor, "The Functionalist Approach to the Problem of International Order: A Defense," *Political Studies*, 16 (October 1968), pp. 393-410; Robert J. Lieber, *Theory and World Politics* (Cambridge, Mass.: Winthrop, 1972); and John J. Weltman, *Systems Theory in International Relations* (Lexington, Mass.: D. C. Health, 1973).

33. Parsons, "Order and Community in the International Social System," in James N. Rosenau (ed.), *International Politics and Foreign Policy*, pp. 120-129. This is not to say that structural-functionalists assume that all domestic societies are fully integrated.

equilibrium of the international system, reveals that these patterns are only in the formative stage. As Talcott Parsons puts it, in referring to "cycles of escalating conflict" that tend to culminate in war:

There are two general reasons why manifestations of strains and underlying conflicts should be more salient in intergroup than in intragroup relations. One is that solidarity is stronger within a group—including a "national" societal community—than between it and others of its type, and therefore there is a tendency to "displace" conflict into the field of intergroup relations. Second, almost by definition, intergroup order is less firmly institution-alized than is intragroup order at corresponding levels, for defenses against the cycles of escalating conflict are weaker.[34]

Even so, structural-functionalists such as Paul Smoker do identify grounds for hope. In an article devoted to an analysis of the arms races that preceded World War I, World War II, and the Cold War, Smoker is able to interpret differences among them in terms of a model which assumes that the international system has become steadily more integrated over time. His conclusions clearly point to a greater and greater chance of controlling the contemporary Soviet-American arms race.[35]

Thus we have seen that structural-functionalists approach an understanding of social reality on three levels: individual, domestic, and international. As firm believers in a benign universe, they assume that properly functioning, homeostatic systems exist (or normally exist) on the first two levels, if not necessarily on the third. In explaining war, therefore, they point either to transitory or momentary malfunctions by individuals or domestic systems, on the one hand, or to the absence of a stable, integrated international system, on the other.

34. Parsons, *The System of Modern Societies*, pp. 140-142. For an earlier version of the Parsonian view of war, see Quincy Wright, *A Study of War* (Chicago: University of Chicago Press, 1964).

35. Paul Smoker, "Nation-State Escalation and International Integra-tion," *Journal of Peace Research*, 4 (1967), pp. 61-74.

③   *Group Conflict Theory*

Scholars on the left of the liberal spectrum have been strongly influenced by various theories of group conflict, particularly those of the German sociologists Georg Simmel (1858-1918) and Max Weber (1869-1920), who insisted that "conflict cannot be excluded from social life."[36] Such theorists generally center their attention *not* on the behavior of individual decision-makers (as do many social-psychologists) or on social systems (as do structural-functionalists), but on struggles among self-serving groups. Lewis Coser (1913-   ) and Ralf Dahrendorf (1929-   ), for example, have objected to functionalism's neglect of conflict and coercion and have argued instead that conflict is a necessary element in the maintenance of social cohesion. In fact, Dahrendorf argues explicitly that the extent of structural change in any system is a function of the relevant "conflict intensity." He thereby rejects Talcott Parsons' structural-functional approach on the grounds that it views conflict as abnormal, deviant, even pathological. Hence, though Dahrendorf may on occasion define himself as a *class* conflict theorist, it is appropriate to discuss his contributions in the context of *group* conflict analysis, for he has shifted the Marxist focus from the *economic relations* of society to the *authority relations* in "imperatively coordinated associations." From his perspective, a radical theory of class conflict based on the division of society into owners and nonowners of the means of production no longer has much analytical value. The more useful category of analysis is "relations of authority," in which some command and others obey, some dominate and others are dominated. In Dahrendorf's opinion, the social system is not primarily maintained by

36. Max Weber, *The Methodology of the Social Sciences*, trans. and ed. by Edward A. Shils and Henry A. Finch (Glencoe, Ill.: Free Press, 1949), p. 26. On Georg Simmel, see his *Conflict* (Glencoe, Ill.: Free Press, 1955); Lewis Coser, *The Functions of Social Conflict* (New York: Free Press, (1956); and Nicholas J. Spykman, *The Social Theory of Georg Simmel* (New York: Atherton Press, 1966).

functional integration by consensus among its constituent parts (the "integration theory of society") but, more generally, is held together by *force* and *constraint* (the "coercion theory of society"). The concept of conflict thus occupies a prominent position in the work of Dahrendorf and other group conflict theorists, and the reality of conflict is viewed by them as having important consequences in terms of structural transformation.[37]

To a greater extent than Marxists, for whom material interests are always paramount, group conflict theorists are prepared to recognize the independent significance of values and ideals in the political sphere of action. In Weberian fashion, they see values as a factor either facilitating or undermining social equilibrium. In this regard, they tend to agree with the structural-functionalists. In another regard, however, they disagree, for from the viewpoint of group conflict theorists, a society does *not* possess one system of values; rather, a society includes many disparate values and ideals, supported by different groups and organizations. Individuals and groups thus have *both* material and ideal interests, each of which may be used as weapons in the political struggle. This is a crucial point for group conflict theorists: ideals and values are themselves *interests*. They

37. See Coser, *The Functions of Social Conflict*; Ralf Dahrendorf, *Class and Class Conflict in Industrial Society* (Stanford, Calif.: Stanford University Press, 1959), pp. 231-235; Dahrendorf, "Toward a Theory of Social Conflict," *Journal of Conflict Resolution*, 2 (June 1958), pp. 170-183; Dahrendorf, *Society and Democracy in Germany* (New York: Doubleday, 1967); and Dahrendorf, *Essays in the Theory of Society* (Stanford, Calif.: Stanford University Press, 1968), especially "In Praise of Thrasymachus," pp. 129-130. On Dahrendorf, see L. E. Hazelrigg, "Class, Property, and Authority: Dahrendorf's Critique of Marx's Theory of Class," *Social Forces*, 50 (June 1972), pp. 473-487; Stanley A. Kockanek, "Perspectives on the Study of Revolution and Social Change," *Comparative Politics*, 5 (April 1973), pp. 315-317; Ted Robert Gurr, "The Revolution-Social Change Nexus," *Comparative Politics*, 5 (April 1973), pp. 372-377, 380; and Joseph Lopreato, "Authority Relations and Class Conflict," in Lopreato and Lionel S. Lewis (eds.), *Social Stratification: A Reader* (New York: Harper and Row, 1974), pp. 252-260.

may exist independently of, and are not necessarily a smoke-screen for, material goals.[38]

If the social world is competitive and conflict-ridden, how is peace achieved, either within a society or among nation-states? Recall that structural-functionalists stress the principle of reciprocity—the existence of mutually beneficial interchanges among interdependent parts (e.g., among nation-states). For group conflict theorists, however, the principle of reciprocity is the exception, not the rule. Power configurations may compel continued interchanges even where no functional reciprocity exists. An organized group, especially a forceful one, may dominate other groups without the groups sharing common values. Group conflict theorists contend, therefore, that social order is achieved through the mutual accommodation of the material and ideal interests of groups and organizations *or* in the domination of some groups over others. According to Ralf Dahrendorf, to repeat, the origin of both conflict and change is in the "dominance relations" characterized by an uneven distribution of power among social groups. Society is thus essentially a network of groups and organizations bound together either by mutuality of interests *or* by dominance and submission.

The logical extension of this approach into the area of international relations involves recognition of the important role played by powerful interest groups and powerful nation-states. But which groups and which nation-states actually foster the policies that lead to war? This was one of the questions addressed by the liberal Austrian economist Joseph Schumpeter (1883-1950) in an essay written in 1919, "The Sociology of Imperialism." In his comparative analysis of past societies, Schumpeter identified particular elite groups whose continued authority and dominance "at home" depended upon warfare. "The orientation toward war is

38. See Randall Collins, "A Comparative Approach to Political Sociology," in Reinhard Bendix (ed.), *State and Society: A Reader in Comparative Sociology* (Boston: Little, Brown, 1968), pp. 48-56.

mainly fostered by the domestic interests of ruling [aristo-
cratic] classes," he contended, "but also by the influence of
all those who stand to gain individually from a war policy,
whether economically or socially."[39] In contrast to Marxist
theorists, Schumpeter rejected the view that the business
bourgeoisie were principally responsible for aggressive foreign policies. Rather, he located the major pressure for
imperialism and war in aristocratic, military, and bureaucratic leaders. Indeed, in his opinion, capitalism is not
warlike when compared with earlier systems: "The competitive system absorbs the full energies of most of the people at
all economic levels. . . . In a purely capitalist world, what
was once energy for war becomes simply energy for labor of
every kind. . . . A purely capitalist world therefore can offer
no fertile soil to imperialist impulses."[40] The bourgeois
leaders of capitalist countries occasionally lead their nations
to war, he conceded, but in such instances they are not
motivated by the imperatives of capitalism. Contemporary
war is neither rational nor self-conscious; it is the result of
atavistic impulses inherited from precapitalist eras. "It
follows," argued Schumpeter, "that it is a basic fallacy to
describe imperialism as a necessary phase of capitalism, or
even to speak of the development of capitalism into imperialism."[41]

A current version of Schumpeter's assertion that traditional elites may seek to preserve their status by stirring up
foreign conflicts can be found in the writings of such people
as Richard Rosecrance, Ernst B. Haas, and Allen S. Whiting. Rosecrance (1930-   ), for example, who employs a kind
of systems analysis more compatible with group conflict
than with structural-functionalist assumptions, argues that
fear and anxiety among decision-making elites whose positions are insecure will contribute to instability in the inter-

39. Joseph Schumpeter, *Imperialism and Social Classes* (New York:
Meridian Books, 1955), p. 65.
40. *Ibid.*, p. 69.
41. *Ibid.*, p. 89.

national system. When decision-makers find themselves threatened internally they are more likely to favor taking aggressive action against other nation-states in order to bolster their position. When, on the other hand, they are secure and essentially satisfied with the status quo, the international system remains relatively stable. During such periods, he maintains, problems will generally be resolved without recourse to war.[42]

Other contemporary scholars of "left-liberal" persuasion, such as Seymour Melman, John Kenneth Galbraith, and Sidney Lens, call our attention to the war-making proclivities of specific interest groups. While some of their conclusions may appear at first glance to be rather radical, upon closer examination the liberal assumptions which govern them emerge clearly. One of these scholars, Seymour Melman (1917-   ), has been among the most ardent critics of the defense establishment and of rising defense budgets in the 1960s and 1970s. In *Our Depleted Society* (1965) and *Pentagon Capitalism* (1970), Melman argued that in the

42. Richard N. Rosecrance, *Action and Reaction in World Politics: International Systems in Perspective* (Boston: Little, Brown, 1963), pp. 304-305; Rosecrance, *International Relations: Peace or War?* (New York: McGraw-Hill, 1973), pp. 23-24. See also Ernst B. Haas and Allen S. Whiting, *Dynamics of International Relations* (New York: McGraw-Hill, 1956), pp. 356-359. Efforts to demonstrate empirically the correlation between elite insecurity and war have had mixed results. Studies showing a positive correlation include Raymond Tanter, "International War and Domestic Turmoil: Some Contemporary Evidence," in Hugh David Graham and Ted Robert Gurr (eds.), *Violence in America: Historical and Comparative Perspectives* (New York: New American Library, 1968), pp. 522-540; Jonathan Wilkenfeld, "Domestic and Foreign Conflict Behavior of Nations," *Journal of Peace Research*, 5 (1968), pp. 50-69; and Wilkenfeld, "Some Further Findings Regarding the Domestic and Foreign Conflict Behavior of Nations," *Journal of Peace Research*, 6 (1969), pp. 147-155. Examinations revealing low correlations between the internal characteristics of states and their aggressive international behavior include Rudolph J. Rummel, "The Relationship between National Attributes and Foreign Conflict Behavior," in J. David Singer (ed.), *Quantitative International Politics: Insights and Evidence* (New York: Free Press, 1968), pp. 187-214; and Melvin Small and J. David Singer, "The War Proneness of Democratic Regimes, 1816-1965," *Jerusalem Journal of International Relations*, 1 (Summer 1976), pp. 50-59.

United States the military was ascendant over the defense industry and that the Department of Defense had become headquarters for a "state-management," a military state within a state. This state-management was viewed by Melman as being an outgrowth of the "military-industrial complex," and, having been created for purposes of national defense, simply thirsted for more and more power. Like Schumpeter before him, Melman rejected the view that capitalism is inherently warlike; like Schumpeter as well, he did not believe that the causes of war (in this case, Vietnam) could be traced to the actions of a business ruling class. For Melman, the coming of war was explained by "an institutionalized power-lust," as distinguished from individual power-lust. What must be reversed, according to him, is the momentum of military institutions. His solution, therefore, is essentially political: dismantle the military-industrial complex and reduce the military.[43]

Likewise, Harvard economist John Kenneth Galbraith (1908-), in a widely read book, *How to Control the Military* (1970), also focused on the bureaucratic, not the economic, dimension:

There have been many explanations of how we got into the Vietnam war. . . . But all the explanations come back to one. It was the result of a long series of steps taken in response to a bureaucratic view of the world—a view to which a President willingly or unwillingly yielded and which, until much too late, was unchecked by any legislative or public opposition.[44]

Elsewhere, Galbraith has argued that "our problem is essentially one of bureaucratic power, of uncontrolled bureaucratic power which, in the manner of all bureaucracies, . . . governs in its own interest."[45] For both Melman and

43. See Seymour Melman, *Our Depleted Society* (New York: Dell, 1965) and *Pentagon Capitalism: The Political Economy of War* (New York: McGraw-Hill, 1970).
44. John Kenneth Galbraith, *How to Control the Military* (New York: Doubleday, 1969). The quotation is from an article by the same title by Galbraith in *Harper's* (June 1969), pp. 32-33.
45. Galbraith, "Scaring the Hell Out of Everybody," *The Progressive,* 33

64 LIBERAL IDEOLOGY AND THEORY

Galbraith, then, the "practice" that flows from their "theory" is action within the political framework "to get the military power under firm political control."

For Sidney Lens (1912-   ), former AFL-CIO labor leader now engaged in independent journalism, in contrast to Melman and Galbraith, the activities of the military-industrial complex must be understood in the context of the global economic needs of the United States. In *The Military-Industrial Complex* (1970), Lens moves close to a radical point of view, portraying this key interest-group as a "conglomerate of elites"—military, industrial, banking, labor, and academic—whose function is global economic expansion to guarantee markets and supplies. This power elite, Lens avers, "would create the international setting in which American private interests could advance unchecked."[46]

We should note, as well, an important group conflict variant of systems theory that conceives of international relations in terms of a struggle for resources within a context of systemic interaction. Proponents of this so-called "stratification approach"—such as Karl Deutsch, J. David Singer, Kenneth Waltz, and Richard Rosecrance—have theorized extensively about the relation between power distributions among the nation-states and the extent of international violence. The earliest analyses, by Deutsch, Singer, and others, were perhaps still close enough to the experience of the early Cold War that they took a very dim view of a bipolar arrangement. Asserting that "as the system moves away from bipolarity toward multipolarity, the frequency of war should be expected to diminish," Deutsch and Singer contended that a multipolar system makes hostility between

---

(June 1969), p. 15. For an interesting discussion of theory attributing major responsibility for foreign policy to organizational (bureaucratic) processes, see Graham T. Allison, *Essence of Decision: Explaining the Cuban Missile Crisis* (Boston: Little, Brown, 1971), pp. 67-143.

46. Sidney Lens, *The Military-Industrial Complex* (Philadelphia: Pilgrim Press, 1970), p. 145. See also pp. 22, 23, and 32.

dyads of nations less probable because it (1) increases the number of cross-cutting loyalties, (2) reduces the amount of attention that any nation can give to any other, and (3) reduces the impact of any nation's arms increases on any other.[47] Subsequent work by other theorists, though clearly based on similar ideological assumptions, was much more sympathetic to bipolarity (perhaps because as a condition it seemed to be passing). Waltz, for instance, maintained that in a nuclear age traditional balance of power expectations must be called into question. Because the two superpowers are alone in having the capacity to inflict and control major destruction, he wrote, they are "able both to moderate others' use of violence and to absorb possibly destabilizing changes that emanate from uses of violence that they do not or cannot control." In a multipolar world which involves nuclear proliferation, satisfactory balances would not be as easy to achieve.[48]

Dissatisfied with both the Deutsch-Singer and Waltz models, Richard Rosecrance offered a third alternative with a system he called bi-multipolarity. What he asserted, in effect, was that under present circumstances both bipolarity and multipolarity possess advantages and disadvantages. Assuming (unlike Deutsch and Singer) that the frequency of conflict is greater in a multipolar world because of a greater diversity of interests and demands, he at the same time suggested that these conflicts will be of much less intensity

47. Karl Deutsch and J. David Singer, "Multipolar Systems and International Stability," *World Politics*, 16 (April 1964), pp. 390-406. See also Morton A. Kaplan, *System and Process in International Politics* (New York: Wiley, 1957). Empirical investigations by Singer and Melvin Small later yielded evidence not completely in support of Singer's earlier hypotheses. For this, see Singer and Small, "Alliance Aggregation and the Onset of War, 1815-1965," in Singer (ed.), *Quantitative International Politics: Insights and Evidence* (New York: Free Press, 1968), pp. 247-286; and Singer and Small, *The Wages of War* (New York: Wiley, 1972).

48. Kenneth N. Waltz, "International Structure, National Force, and the Balance of World Power," *Journal of International Affairs*, 21 (1967), pp. 215-231. See also Waltz, "The Stability of the Bipolar World," *Daedalus*, 93 (Summer 1964), pp. 881-909.

than in a bipolar structure. On the other hand, while bipolarity may involve a serious conflict between the two poles, it also reduces or eliminates conflict elsewhere in the system. With Rosecrance's own arrangement (bi-multipolarity), by contrast, "the two major states would act as regulators for conflict in the external areas; but multipolar states would act as mediators and buffers for conflict between the bipolar powers."[49]

(Parenthetically, we would point out—something those versed in American history may well have already noted—that the disagreements among these systems theorists are reminiscent of an analogous debate that occurred, some 65 years ago, between the liberal theoreticians of the Progressive era, Louis Brandeis and Herbert Croly. In that instance, when the issue at hand was what to do with the giant corporations that were destroying the rights of the small entrepreneurs, Brandeis spoke out unequivocally for breaking them apart in the name of "healthy" competition, while Croly was much more willing to retain them and gain what advantages they could give, as long as they were balanced in

49. Richard N. Rosecrance, "Bipolarity, Multipolarity, and the Future," *Journal of Conflict Resolution*, 10 (September 1966), pp. 314-327. For a similar "multi-hierarchical" approach to stratification, see Stanley Hoffman, *Gulliver's Troubles, Or the Setting of American Foreign Policy* (New York: McGraw-Hill, 1968). For general discussion, see Dougherty and Pfaltzgraff, *Contending Theories of International Relations*, pp. 130-134; Patrick M. Morgan, *Theories and Approaches to International Politics* (San Ramon, Calif.: Consensus Publishers, 1975), pp. 245-248; and Michael Haas, *International Conflict* (New York: Bobbs-Merrill, 1974), pp. 317-323.

In a clarifying letter to the authors (May 4, 1977), Michael Haas writes: "The 'stratification' and 'community' approaches are *approaches*, not *metatheories*. An approach has a conceptual framework but no integrated set of testable propositions. A metatheory has both. Those who use the stratification approach postulate one simple proposition, namely, that warfare is more or less likely, depending upon power configurations of the actors in an international system. The community approach stresses international linkages as predictors to war and peace. . . . Yes, the 'conflict approach' is implicit in the stratification approach, whereas a 'consensus approach' is implicit in the community approach as well as in Parsons' structural-functional metatheory."

the end by other elements equally powerful. Thus, in Croly's case, as with Waltz, there was a tendency for the sake of efficiency to move surprisingly near a conservative position, with power concentrated in a few hands.[50])

In summary, then, the major analytical concepts of group conflict theory are the material and ideal interests of individuals, and of those groups and organizations created by individuals to pursue those interests. The political process is not viewed in structural-functional terms as meeting the interests of society as a whole, nor in Marxist terms as serving the interests of a ruling class. Rather, it is seen in group conflict terms as reflecting the continuous struggle for political advantage, both within and among nation-states. This struggle is said to be carried on, to a great extent, under conditions of coercion and domination. Furthermore, the political and economic spheres are viewed as independent but interacting, and, in very non-Marxist fashion, are deemed to be analytically distinct. The outcomes of the political struggles among groups, as Randall Collins puts it, "are not solely or preponderantly determined by the relationships of groups to the economic structure, as in Marxist theory."[51]

CONCLUSION

We would emphasize that the fear of bureaucratic power characteristic of much liberal theory is completely in accord with one of the major tenets of liberal ideology—namely, a longstanding concern about "big government" as a major source of the problems confronting society. It was, after all, against government that liberal theory first arose. Nevertheless, we have seen that liberal theories about war reflect a

50. On this, see Arthur S. Link, *Woodrow Wilson and the Progressive Era, 1910-1917* (New York: Harper and Row, 1954), pp. 18-22.

51. Randall Collins, "A Comparative Approach to Political Sociology," pp. 49-50. See also Collins, *Conflict Sociology: Toward an Explanatory Science* (New York: Academic Press, 1975), pp. 49-89.

spectrum of opinion regarding human behavior ranging from a belief that liberal nation-states behave rationally and cooperatively unless their leaders and citizens fall victim to misperceptions and stereotypes (social-psychological theory), to a view that systems are more often functionally interdependent at the national than the international level (structural-functionalism), to an assertion that both domestic and international systems are comprised of competing groups and therefore require internal coercion and balancing of power (group conflict theory). As we shall discover in the next chapter, this stress on tension among groups becomes even more pronounced in radical theory about society and war.

CHAPTER THREE

Radical Ideology and Theory about the Causes of War

THE RADICAL TRADITION

Radicalism, like liberalism, is an exceedingly complex ideology that draws inspiration from a variety of sources. Both liberalism and radicalism have been what the sociologist C. Wright Mills called "insurgent creeds," serving as the "rhetoric of movements, parties and classes on the road to power."[1] Historically, especially in Northern Europe and the United States, liberalism has been the ideology of the rising urban and entrepreneurial middle classes of advancing capitalist societies, while radicalism has been the guiding ideology for working-class movements and parties. Radicals have generally endorsed the liberal ideas of freedom and equality inherited from the Enlightenment, but, as early as

1. C. Wright Mills, *The Marxists* (New York: Dell, 1962), p. 19. We note here that some might wish to equate radicalism with political movements, either Right or Left, that employ violent means to achieve their ends. Such an instrumental definition poses serious problems, however, for not only have extremist methods been used on occasion by conservatives and liberals, but, in addition, peaceful means have been utilized by many radicals, including those of Marxist persuasion. As we have intimated before, we believe that it is more useful to discuss ideology in the full breadth of its tradition than in a narrow instrumental sense. Contextual situations (and political tactics) change rapidly, but idea systems have a marvelous inertia (which is *not* to say that an environment may not ultimately alter an ideology, as, for example, the arrival of the age of atomic weapons has subtly affected Marxist attitudes and thought).

69

Jean Jacques Rousseau (1712-1778), have strongly disagreed with liberals about the meaning of those terms and about the material conditions under which "true" freedom and equality can be manifested and more broadly experienced. Rousseau, for example, formulated a "social contract," not between the ruler and the ruled, but among *the people themselves as equals*, who could thereby commit their passions to the more complete realization of a democratic ideal.

Of radicalism's major components, perhaps the most basic is a *critical analysis of the existing social order as a whole* or of one or more of its institutions. A second component is a *program of social change* designed to destroy or fundamentally transform that social order or certain of its institutions in favor of something more egalitarian in terms both of material rewards and power relationships. These components generally entail a firm rejection of the belief that only a select few have the wisdom, right, and power to govern. Instead, radicals struggle for the masses against the elites, for the underprivileged against the privileged, for the workers against the owners. In contradistinction to the conservative's pessimistic view of human nature (though not to the liberal's optimistic one) is the radical's assumption that *man is fundamentally a rational being fully capable of comprehending social reality* and *joining with others to control the physical and social environment for human betterment*. Radicals, in short, urge us to abandon Hobbes and Locke for Rousseau, and to search first for human freedom and brotherhood, not social stability or individualism.[2]

Curiously, given the ideological distance between radicals and conservatives, there has been substantial accord between these two groups in emphasizing the negative conse-

2. For general descriptions of radicalism, see the essays by Horace M. Kallen in the *Encyclopedia of the Social Sciences*, 13 (New York: Macmillan, 1934), pp. 52-54; and Egon Bittner in the *International Encylopedia of the Social Sciences*, 13 (New York: Macmillan, 1968), pp. 294-299.

quences of modernization and industrialization: the degra-
dation and poverty of workers; the fragmentation and
atomization of social relationships; the destruction of old
ways of life without satisfactory replacements; the rise to
power of industrial and finance capitalists. On one important issue, however, the radical position is in direct opposition to that of conservatives and liberals alike: that regarding the preservation of private property. For both conservatives and liberals, property (whether in the form of land or
capital) is a foundation of the social order and its protection
is considered to be of paramount importance. For conservatives especially, the essence of property is its unequal distribution. For radicals, on the other hand, *the influence of
private property is so pernicious and divisive that its
abolition is absolutely essential.* For this reason radicals
reject the assumption, shared by conservatives and liberals,
*that capitalism is the economic system best able to protect
individual rights and to advance the cause of individual
freedom.* Rather, they see the potential for a more free and
rational society blocked by the structure of capitalism.

Not always

We have seen how conservatives have affirmed the authority of the hierarchical community and how liberals have
asserted the authority of the autonomous individual. Radicals counter by pointing to the dominance (though not the
desirability) of *the social class*, as distinguished from earlier
concepts of social hierarchy. Karl Marx (1813-1883), for
example, argued that the most important principle of social
organization is the class structure, defining different classes
by their relation to the essential means of production. He
viewed class conflict as the motor for social evolution. Syn-
dicalism, Fabianism, guild socialism, Marxian communism
and many other radical movements of the nineteenth century took as their starting point the existence of class.

This concept of class is closely related to another characteristic of the radical tradition that (except in its utopian and
anarchist versions) departs from the main line of conservative and liberal thought—its *recourse to political power as a*

CLASS

means of achieving a more just social order. This attitude toward power, it should be pointed out, is not a blind faith in power for its own sake. Rather, power is to be used to achieve the humanitarian and rationalist *liberation of men and women from their exploitation and alienation.* Marxist theory, for instance, defines political power as "the organized power of one class for oppressing another," and predicts that once power has been utilized by the working class to obliterate class distinctions and to "level" society, it will then disappear.

No other aspect of Marxist thought has been so distorted and misunderstood as its theory of the state and political power. It was Marx's contention that the state is a transitory phenomenon, an artificial creation superimposed on society in order to fulfill certain functions that are socially necessary during a given epoch. *The capitalist state*, which Marx identified with the rise of private property, was seen *primarily* as *a creature of the capitalist class.* "The executive of the modern state," he declared in *The Communist Manifesto* (1848), "is but a committee for managing the common affairs of the whole bourgeoisie."[3] For most Marxists, particularly Marxist-Leninists, it is imperative that the working class in capitalist societies destroy the existing coercive state by revolutionary means and then create its own, to exist during the long transition stage of socialism. This new proletarian state is to endure until the necessary state functions (e.g., centralized planning of the economy) are assumed by new social institutions. When a

3. Karl Marx, *The Communist Manifesto* (New York: International Publishers, 1932), pp. 8-9. On Marx's theory of the state and political power, see Henri Lefebvre, *The Sociology of Marx* (New York: Pantheon Books, 1968), Chap. 5; Robert C. Tucker, *The Marxian Revolutionary Idea* (New York: North, 1969), Chap. 3; Ralph Miliband, *The State in Capitalist Society* (New York: Basic Books, 1969); and Ernesto Laclau, "The Specificity of the Political: The Poulantzas-Miliband Debate," *Economy and Society*, 4 (February 1975), pp. 87-110. For a very instructive discussion of the views of Lenin and Weber on such issues, see Erik Olin Wright, "To Control or To Smash Bureaucracy: Weber and Lenin on Politics, the State, and Bureaucracy," *Berkeley Journal of Sociology*, 19 (1974-1975), pp. 69-108.

truly rational organization of production becomes possible in a communist society, the state will begin to "wither away." When classes are abolished, repressive institutions will become unnecessary and human freedom (defined by Marx as the ability to shape and control one's destiny and to maximize one's inherent potentialities) will be fully realized.[4]

Marxian radicalism is thus ultimately anti-statist, having inherited from liberalism the belief that the role of the state should be reduced to a minimum. Indeed, Marx's normative position with regard to the state was almost anarchist, embodying the view that state power can never be legitimized. As Marxist philosopher Henri Lefebvre has pointed out, Marx viewed the purpose of revolutionary struggle "as to go beyond democracy and beyond the democratic state, to build a society without state power."[5] In short, Marx envisioned the time when the "people" would assume control and direction of the economy, without bureaucracy or the state. Where he differed from anarchists like Georges Sorel (1847-1922) was in his temporary reliance on the state to overthrow the capitalist class, something the anarchists did not believe was necessary.[6]

This description of the basic premises of radical ideology

4. For a description of the process by which the state will "wither away," see Frederick Engels' *Anti-Dühring* (1877), as quoted in Emile Burns (ed.), *A Handbook of Marxism* (New York: Random House, 1935), pp. 295-296.

5. See Lefebvre, *The Sociology of Marx*, pp. 123-125, and Tucker, *The Marxian Revolutionary Idea*, pp. 85-91.

6. The sociologist Max Weber is usually given credit for developing the first critique of the function of bureaucracy in the modern state, although Marx (in his critical notes on Hegel's philosophy of the state) anticipated Weber in this regard. Even before World War I Weber argued cogently that the satisfaction of human needs under conditions of socialism would undoubtedly require an *increase* of industrialization and centralized planning, an augmentation rather than a diminution of the powers of the state—and thus an intensification of bureaucratic domination. It would not be possible, according to Weber, to have both affluence *and* freedom; it would be necessary to choose between the two. See Jean Cohen, "Max Weber and the Dynamics of Rationalized Domination," *Telos*, 14 (Winter 1972), pp. 78, 80-82. See also Reinhard Bendix, *Max Weber: An Intellec-*

is much too brief to delineate clearly the many variations within that tradition. Among competing interpreters, for example, are Marxist-Leninists, Maoists, Social-Democrats (or "revisionist" socialists), and what social critic Peter Clecak has called the "plain Marxists" (i.e., independent intellectuals such as the Frankfurt School, C. Wright Mills, or Herbert Marcuse).[7] We have stressed the enormous influence of Karl Marx in the formulation of radical ideology, primarily because Marxism-Leninism possesses the most fully elaborated theory of war. It is the theory against which rival radical theories (both Marxist and anarchist) have defined themselves.

Despite the theoretical differences and often intense polemical battles that divide radicals, there are yet some common premises that serve to unite them: a *critical evaluation of the existing social order* combined with a *program designed to transform that order in humanitarian and democratic directions*; a *view of man as fundamentally rational* and capable of exercising control over the physical and social environment; a *rejection of private property and capitalism*; a *belief in the importance of social class* and (for revolutionary Marxists, at least) of the continuous class struggle to achieve human liberation from exploitation and alienation; a *reliance on political power to overthrow the coercive state*; and a *condemnation of liberals* for failing to achieve their proclaimed ideals in practice. These basic tenets inform various radical theories of war, to which we now turn.

RADICAL THEORY ABOUT THE CAUSES OF WAR

Radical analyses of war place even greater stress than do liberal theories on the connection between domestic struc-

tual Portrait (New York: Anchor Books, 1962), especially Chaps. 7 and 8 on the concept of "legal domination"; and Kostas Papaioannou, "Marx and the Bureaucratic State," *Dissent* (May-June 1969), pp. 252-262.

7. See Peter Clecak, *Radical Paradoxes: Dilemmas of the American Left, 1945-1970* (New York: Harper and Row, 1973). pp. 17-20.

tures and international conflict. Radicals, of course, are intensely critical of prevailing social conditions, the responsibility for which they attribute not to individuals, but to structural factors. Those basic structures and institutions, in their view, are essentially impervious to change except through conflict instigated by social groups. They are therefore deeply interested in the mutual interaction of international conflict and domestic struggles for social change.

Radical theorists tend to reject both the conservative notion that there is something innately aggressive about man and the liberal view that events may be explained primarily in psychological terms or in terms of a breakdown of accommodating structures or balanced systems. In particular, they are not persuaded by liberal arguments based on individual personality, psychological stress on major decision-makers, "crisis mentality," "war fever" generated by the press, and so forth. Recall that the "situational analysis" of many liberal theorists assumes that the action of decision-makers is a function of the immediate situation, of the crisis itself (e.g., World War I occurred because the international crisis of July 1914 was mismanaged diplomatically). For radicals, however, events are only intelligible in terms of social structures beyond the *immediate* control of human actors. Rousseau, for example, concluded that property ownership was the root cause of war and argued that wars would end only when private property was abolished.[8] In similar fashion, "utopian" socialists of the early nineteenth century, such as Count Saint-Simon, Robert Owen, Charles Fourier, and John Humphrey Noyes, all described war as a manifestation of the capitalist system. Karl Marx offered an explanation of social action not in terms of how individuals thought of themselves (as in the status-anxiety

8. See Jean Jacques Rousseau, *Discourse on the Origin of Inequality*, (New York: E. P. Dutton, 1941), p. 213 and his 1731 essay, *A Project of Perpetual Peace*, translated by Edith M. Nutall (London: Cobden-Sanderson, 1927). See also Stanley Hoffmann, "Rousseau on War and Peace," *American Political Science Review*, 57 (June 1963), pp. 317-333.

hypothesis of liberal theorists), but rather in terms of their objective relation to the economic system of a given society: "It is not the consciousness of men which determines their existence, but on the contrary it is their social existence which determines their consciousness."[9]

Radical theorists, therefore, while not denying the role of human will, are more likely to accept notions of "limited choice," arguing that the real causes of international conflict lie in long-term factors such as economic competition, imperialism, nationalism, racism, and the like. Radicals perceive that these factors severely limit the options of international leaders in periods of crisis. This does not mean, however, that policy is viewed as an emotional, irrational reaction to historical circumstances, but rather is seen as the rational, calculated, premeditated response of a ruling class or elite to significant domestic or foreign developments. Thus, in radical theory about war, the behavior of the leaders during times of crisis is largely determined by pre-crisis conditions.[10]

The most systematic radical theory of war (and the leading exemplar of revolutionary, or "orthodox," class conflict theory) is the Marxist-Leninist, which explains modern international conflict as the inevitable result of capitalism having reached its monopoly, and therefore imperialist, stage. Its principal theoretical rival, which derives from evolutionary, or "revisionist," class conflict theory and is usually labeled socialist or Social Democratic,

9. Karl Marx, from the introduction to *Critique of Political Economy* (1857), reprinted in Max Eastman (ed.), *Capital and Other Writings by Karl Marx* (New York: Modern Library, 1932), p. 11.

10. See L. L. Farrar, Jr., "The Limits of Choice: July 1914 Reconsidered," *Journal of Conflict Resolution*, 16 (March 1972), pp. 5-6. As Mao Tse-tung declared at the meeting of the Supreme Soviet of the U.S.S.R. on November 6, 1957: "The socialist system will replace the capitalist system in the end. This is an objective law independent of human will. No matter how hard the reactionaries try to prevent the wheel of history from advancing, revolution will take place sooner or later and will surely triumph." See K. Fan (ed.), *Mao Tse-tung and Lin Piao: Post-Revolutionary Writings* (New York: Anchor Books, 1972), p. 223.

does not offer the same precision or coherency as Marxism-Leninism, perhaps in part because it has no dominating representative. Social Democratic theorists and historians, in attempting to chart an independent path between territory occupied by "naive" liberals, on the one side, and "determinist" Marxists, on the other, draw in an eclectic and sometimes contradictory manner from both. Revisionist theory retains Marxist notions of class and a belief in the provocative nature of capitalism, but it tends to define class more loosely than the Marxist-Leninists and at times shades off into ideas compatible with group conflict liberalism.

"Orthodox" Class Conflict Theory

Traditionally, Marxist theorists begin with a view of society in capitalist nations as a series of interacting horizontal levels, or social groupings. They argue that in such societies there is a continuous conflict, arising from the social division of labor, between two basic classes: the bourgeoisie (which owns and controls the means of production—capital, machines, raw materials) and the proletariat (a productive force that owns nothing except its own labor, which it is "free" to sell to the capitalist owners of the means of production).[11] The proletariat is constantly engaged in resisting exploitation by the bourgeoisie, although the struggle is not always carried on at the same level of intensity. The possessing classes, utilizing the coercive power of the state, attempt to thwart the efforts of the producing class to transform society. As we have seen, certain social-psychological explanations of historical change hold that status groups compete for the distribution of prestige and the allocation of *social status*. Marxist theory, on the other hand, focuses on classes, not individuals or groups, and argues that classes are economically oriented, being concerned primarily with the distribution of *material resources*.

11. See Ernest Mandel, *An Introduction to Marxist Theory* (New York: Merit Publishers, 1968), pp. 31-34.

Class struggle and conflict, not order and consensus, are thus the normal conditions of social life in capitalist society. This Marxist conception of modern society is very different from the conservative's, who admires traditional society because of the obligations linking all members of the community and who decries the forces of modernization for transmitting power from those occupying the upper ranks of a social hierarchy to the masses on the bottom. The Marxist conception also differs markedly from the structural-functional liberal's, who conceives of society as a set of interdependent parts, or from the group conflict liberal's, for whom organized interest groups (not social classes) are the dominant reality. As far as the latter are concerned, these interest groups compete and collide, but no single group ever dominates for long. Such a conception, from the point of view of the Marxist, is a serious distortion of the way things are.

The Marxist stress on conflict is just as pronounced in the analysis of international relations as it is in domestic politics. According to this perspective, those who control the economic system also control the political system and, logically, the decisions that flow from that system, including the decision to go to war. Marxism thus approaches foreign policy and domestic policy as an organic unity, as parts of the overall policy pursued by the ruling class of the state. In the Marxist view, the cause of war is the very existence of a class society.

Nevertheless, though Marx was well informed about the worldwide scope of capitalist activities, he never formulated a systematic theory of imperialism or of war. That task was performed by his intellectual successors—Rudolf Hilferding (1877-1941), Rosa Luxembourg (1870-1919), and especially V. I. Lenin (1870-1923). Lenin himself profited from the work of a British economist and reformer, J. A. Hobson (1858-1940).

Hobson certainly had no great sympathy for the Marxists, but in his analysis of the capitalist system (published in

1902) he argued in Marxist fashion that capitalism faced an internal and critical difficulty: the unequal distribution of wealth. A few capitalists were accumulating great surplus wealth, he contended, while the impoverished majority lacked the purchasing power to participate actively as consumers. Because the capitalists were not willing to redistribute their wealth by paying workers higher wages, they were compelled to reinvest it elsewhere. Hobson's critique thus stressed the importance of underconsumption at home and investment of surplus capital in profitable ventures abroad. The result of these foreign involvements was imperialism, by means of which capitalists were ensuring their economic survival. Furthermore, the search for foreign markets was leading directly to competition and struggle among nations, and in this manner imperialism was becoming a road to war. From Hobson's left liberal perspective, it is important to note, the conflict resulting from imperialism (as well as imperialism itself) was viewed as a deplorable mistake that could be avoided with appropriate corrective measures. He even expressed the hope that rival imperialisms might establish working agreements so as to avoid war among themselves.[12]

Though Hobson's theory of imperialism and war was regarded as outrageous by most economists of his day, it was taken very seriously by the Marxists. German socialist Rosa Luxembourg's definition of imperialism was quite similar to that of Hobson: "the political expression of the accumulation of capital in its competitive struggle for what remains still open of the non-capitalist environment."[13] Yet in Luxembourg's hands Hobson's argument was rendered

12. John A. Hobson, *Imperialism: A Study* (London: George Allen and Unwin, 1902), pp. 15-86, 207-234. See also Robert L. Heilbroner, *The Worldly Philosophers* (New York: Simon and Schuster, 1961), pp. 168-170. For an application of some of Hobson's conclusions to the contemporary world, see Michael Hudson, *Super-Imperialism: The Economic Strategy of American Empire* (New York: Holt, Rinehart and Winston, 1972).

13. Rosa Luxembourg, *The Accumulation of Capital* (London: Routledge, 1955; first published in 1913), p. 446.

both more impersonal and more inexorable. And she certainly rejected Hobson's earnest hope that imperialist nation-states might arrange to coexist peaceably. Rudolf Hilferding, an economist and one of the leaders of the radical wing of the Socialist party in Germany, augmented the theories of Hobson and Luxembourg by establishing a link between the export of capital and the operation of systems dominated by monopolies and cartels.[14] Finally, to complete the evolution of thought, V. I. Lenin in the years of the First World War constructed a theory of imperialism that incorporated basic elements from the analyses of Hobson, Luxembourg, and Hilferding:

> Imperialism is capitalism in that stage of development in which the domination of monopolies and finance capital has established itself; in which the export of capital has acquired pronounced importance; in which the division of the world among the international trusts has begun; in which the division of all territories of the globe among the great capitalist powers has been completed.[15]

Lenin

For Lenin, then, as for subsequent theorists in the Marxist-Leninist tradition, imperialism is equated with the development of monopoly capitalism (in which "free enterprise" capitalism has been superseded by increasing concentration and centralization of capital in fewer and fewer hands) beyond the boundaries of the nation-state. Imperialism is *not* a preferred "foreign policy" developed by capitalists and capable of being abandoned by them, as Lenin's socialist rival Karl Kautsky (1854-1938) argued. Quite the contrary.

14. Rudolf Hilferding, *Das Finanzkapital: Eine Studie über die jüngste Entwicklung des Kapitalismus* (Vienna: I. Brand, 1910).

15. V. I. Lenin, *Imperialism: The Highest Stage of Capitalism* (New York: International Publishers, 1939; first published in 1916), p. 89; and *Lenin on War and Peace* (Peking: Foreign Language Press, 1966; first published in 1915-1924). See also Karel Kara, "On the Marxist Theory of War and Peace," *Journal of Peace Research*, 5 (1968), pp. 1-27. For an explanation of imperialism similar to Lenin's, see Nikolai Bukharin, *Imperialism and World Economy* (New York: Monthly Review Press, 1973; first published in 1917); and Stephen F. Cohen, *Bukharin and the Bolshevik Revolution: A Political Biography, 1888-1938* (New York: Vintage Books, 1975), Chap. 1.

Imperialism is an economic reality, a special, advanced stage of capitalism itself, not amenable to change by the capitalists. Unlike Kautsky, Lenin did not believe that the capitalist nations could cooperate in the exploitation of the underdeveloped world. Instead, wars would inevitably result from increasingly acute competition among capitalist nations in their continual search for cheap raw materials, markets for commodities and for excess capital, and cheap labor.

For Marxist-Leninist theorists, therefore, modern war is a function of capitalist imperialism and a consequence of domestic class struggle. For them the abolition of international conflict requires the elimination of capitalism as the economic system of major nation-states. There is in Marxist-Leninist theory (at least until the end of the Stalin era) no such thing as a real choice, since the development of imperialism and war under capitalism has been seen as inexorable. It has been assumed that a grave danger of war will persist until a classless and stateless communist order is universally established.[16]

16. Another class conflict analysis, the Trotskyist theory of imperialism, deserves brief mention. While both Lenin and his fellow revolutionist Leon Trotsky (1877-1940) acknowledged the importance of imperialism in relation to war, their respective analyses differed in emphasis, with Trotsky stressing the manner in which capitalism had penetrated the underdeveloped world and Lenin denying such penetration. For our purposes, however, their points of agreement are more important than their disagreements, for they were as one in viewing World War I as the result of struggles among capitalists for access to raw materials, markets, and investment opportunities. On Trotsky, see his *Voina i Revolyutsiya*, 2 vols. (Moscow, 1923), pp. 75-76, as quoted in Richard B. Day, *Leon Trotsky and the Politics of Economic Isolation* (Cambridge, Eng.: Cambridge University Press, 1973), p. 13; Trotsky, *The Bolsheviki and World Peace* (New York: Boni and Liveright, 1918), as quoted in Isaac Deutscher (ed.), *The Age of Permanent Revolution: A Trotsky Anthology* (New York: Dell, 1964), pp. 71-72; Trotsky, *Results and Prospects and the Permanent Revolution* (New York: Pathfinder Press, 1969), pp. 278-279; and Baruch Knei-Paz, *The Social and Political Thought of Leon Trotsky* (Oxford: Oxford University Press, 1977). For a Marxist-Leninist criticism of the Trotskyist position, see David J. Romagnolo, "The So-Called 'Law' of Uneven and Combined Development," *Latin American Perspectives*, 2 (Spring 1975), pp. 1-28. For a leading contemporary statement of the Trotskyist position, see Ernest Mandel, *Marxist Economy Theory*, 2 vols. (New York: Monthly Review Press, 1968), Vol. 2, Chap. 13.

Since the 1950s and 1960s, however, a body of Marxist-Leninist doctrine has emerged in the Soviet Union that has considerably altered Lenin's earlier concepts. The major expression of this reapplication of Marxist-Leninist methodology and analysis is to be found in several recent Soviet military textbooks. Not surprisingly, in these publications international monopoly capitalism and imperialism continue to be viewed as reactionary and aggressive. Indeed, the danger they pose to peace, the Soviet writers argue, has been exacerbated in the post-World War II era by the growing "influence of the so-called military-industrial complex—an alliance of the largest monopolies with the military in the state apparatus." These new monopolies "comprise the economic basis [for] the unabated arms race, for preparing for and starting a war . . . , for increasing tension throughout the world, and for supporting adventuristic military dictatorships and fascist regimes." Furthermore, according to these Soviet military spokesmen, with the development of nuclear weapons after 1945 America entered upon a new stage of imperialism in which weapons of mass destruction were being designed for use against the Soviet Union and other socialist nations. Only the development of similar weaponry by the Russians prevented this policy from being implemented, with the result that the United States was forced to adopt a strategy of "flexible response" (aimed at conducting aggressive "limited" and local wars with both conventional and tactical nuclear weapons). This new policy ensured continuing profits for American military manufacturers and was designed to strengthen international capitalism without resort to catastrophic thermonuclear war.[17]

17. See, for example, Col. Gen. N. A. Lomov (ed.), *Scientific-Technical Progress and The Revolution in Military Affairs* (Moscow: Military Publishing House, Ministry of Defense, 1973), trans. and pubd. under the auspices of the United States Air Force (Washington, D.C.: U.S. Government Printing Office, n.d.), pp. 251-256; and Gen. Maj. A. S. Milovidov and Col. V. G. Koslov (eds.), *The Philosophical Heritage of V. I. Lenin and Problems of Contemporary War* (Moscow: Military Publishing House, Ministry of Defense, 1972), trans. and pub. under the auspices of the

Military – Industrial Complex

Thus an important component of the new Soviet theory of war rejects Lenin's (and, subsequently, Stalin's) notions regarding the inevitability of war: "The time is long past when world wars caused by the existence of imperialism were inevitable." Instead, because of the "vigorous, correct" foreign policies of the U.S.S.R. and other socialist nations, most of the world has enjoyed peace for a comparatively long time. With the growing strength of the Soviet Union and the socialist bloc, and with the increasing concern about the destructiveness of nuclear weapons, the prospects for continued peace will improve.[18]

A number of American Marxists, including Paul Baran, Paul Sweezy, and Victor Perlo, have also emphasized the role of the military-industrial complex and the importance of military spending as a means to counter the economic stagnation inherent in capitalism. Still, these radical scholars, unlike the liberal group conflict theorists discussed in Chapter 2, link war and militarism directly with capitalism. Victor Perlo, for example, contends that "wars under capitalism create an extraordinary demand for basic industrial products and stimulate economic growth by releasing potentials that are otherwise suppressed by the contradictions of the system."[19]

Finally, before turning from orthodox class conflict the-

United States Air Force (Washington, D.C.: U.S. Government Printing Office, n.d.), pp. 16-17.

18. See Milovidov and Kozlov (eds.), *The Philosophical Heritage of V. I. Lenin*, pp. 17-19. For extremely useful general treatments, see *Marxism-Leninism on War and Army* (Moscow: Military Publishing House, Ministry of Defense, 1972), trans. and pub. under the auspices of the United States Air Force (Washington, D.C.: U.S. Government Printing Office, n.d.); and P. H. Vigor, *The Soviet View of War, Peace and Neutrality* (London and Boston: Routledge and Kegan Paul, 1975). See also P. H. Vigor and John Erickson, "The Soviet View of the Theory and Strategy of War," *RUSI* (Journal of the Royal United Services Institute for Defense Studies), 115 (June 1970), pp. 3-13.

19. See Victor Perlo, *The Unstable Economy: Booms and Recessions in the U.S. Since 1945* (New York: International Publishers, 1973), p. 169. See also Paul A. Baran and Paul M. Sweezy, *Monopoly Capital* (New York: Monthly Review Press, 1968), Chap. 7.

ory, mention should be made of the Maoist adaptation of Marxism-Leninism to Chinese traditions and experience. Mao Tse-tung (1883-1976), Lenin's counterpart as leader of the Chinese Revolution of 1947-1949, insisted that Marxism must take on a national form before it can be applied. While Mao's theory of imperialism and war closely resembles that of earlier Marxist-Leninists, there is a distinct Maoist tendency to identify imperialism with *both* the Western capitalist nations and the Soviet Union. The dichotomy that emerges in Maoist theory is that of Western imperialism versus the Third World, a kind of North-South axis to replace the East-West battlelines of the Cold War period. While Mao continues to stress the vanguard role of the proletariat, the most important emphasis in his thought is upon the revolutionary potential of the peasantries of the Third World. The Maoist expectation is that Asia, Africa, and Latin America will constitute "the storm center of the world revolution." The Soviet Union, on the other hand, having abandoned Leninism for national aggrandizement, now constitutes a major threat to peace and an obstacle to revolution. And unlike contemporary Soviet theorists of war, Maoists still retain the original Leninist position regarding the inevitability of war in the age of imperialism.[20]

"Revisionist" Class Conflict Theory

As we have seen, the serious application of Marxist economic theory to the problems of imperialism and war did not begin until the turn of the twentieth century. In subsequent years, Marxist as well as other radicals found themselves disagreeing sharply about the causes of these phe-

20. See, among others, Stuart R. Schram, *The Political Thought of Mao Tse-tung* (New York: Frederick A. Praeger, 1969), pp. 100-103, 134-138, 172; Hélène Carrère d'Encausse and Stuart R. Schram, *Marxism and Asia* (London: Allen Lane, Penguin Press, 1969), pp. vii-ix, 102-112; and Philippe Devillers, *Mao* (New York: Schocken Books, 1969), Chap. 11. See also Alexander Atkinson, "Chinese Communist Strategic Thought: The Strategic Premise of Protracted War," *RUSI* (Journal of the Royal United Services Institute for Defense Studies), 118 (March 1973), pp. 60-64.

nomena. For this reason, some familiarity with the issues involved in the intense theoretical debates and political struggles between "orthodox" Marxists and "revisionist" Marxists during this period is most helpful in understanding the revisionist theory of war, and how it differs from Marxist-Leninist theory.

To the great consternation of Karl Marx, the European socialist parties that emerged in the 1870s and 1880s often sponsored political programs that departed from his own analysis of capitalist economic development, the necessity for revolution, and the class character of the state. By the 1890s such parties had become the scene of recurrent battles between followers of older doctrine and those who were coming to be known as "revisionist" socialists. These revisionists, led in Germany by Eduard Bernstein (1850-1932) and in France by Jean Jaurès (1859-1914), took a much "softer" position than their opponents on the necessity of class conflict, arguing that it might not be absolutely inevitable. In their view, capitalism might gradually be transformed in the workers' interest through democratic means, without revolution and without a dictatorship of the proletariat. This optimistic (as opposed to "imminent collapse") theory of capitalist development required Bernstein to abandon dialectical materialism with its assertion that socialism would result inevitably from the demise of capitalism. On the contrary, Bernstein argued, socialism would come about only through conscious, rational decisions. Favorable prospects for socialism required capitalist prosperity, not capitalist collapse. The real enemy of the working class was not capitalism itself, but the self-serving private interests that stubbornly resisted progressive change. The way to destroy the power of this small group of selfish men was not revolution, but political democracy.[21]

21. See Carl E. Schorske, *German Social Democracy, 1905-1917* (New York: Wiley, 1965), pp. 16-20. Schorske writes (p. 20) that Bernstein "had replaced a capitalism proceeding through contradiction to its own destruction with a capitalism moving through prosperity to a higher form of

Understandably, these revisionist notions were bitterly denounced by "orthodox," revolutionary Marxists. In Germany, for example, Karl Kautsky, the intellectual leader of the Socialist party, rejected Bernstein's analysis, arguing instead that the inherent contradictions in capitalism, far from abating, were in fact intensifying. In 1903, at a party congress of the Russian socialists, Lenin demanded that revisionism be firmly quashed and that a small, elite, centralized party be established. He convinced a majority of the delegates to support this Bolshevik position, while those revisionist Marxists who desired a more open, less professional party, and who were willing to work with bourgeois liberals, became known as Mensheviks.

Despite his early opposition to revisionism, Kautsky himself ultimately became highly skeptical about the revolutionary potential of the working class. In *The Road to Power* (1909), he contended that revolution would indeed be an inevitable product of capitalist development, yet he assigned a very passive role to the working class and to its party. The proletariat was to organize and agitate, but the ruling class, through its own incompetence and moral corruption, would provide the key to the destruction of the existing order.[22]

Kautsky's departure from orthodox Marxist theory was not limited to these views of the working class but extended to his explanation of imperialism and war. In the years immediately preceding the outbreak of World War I, Kautsky presented an interpretation of imperialism very different from Lenin's. (Indeed, it was Kautsky's article on this subject in 1914 that provoked Lenin to write his classic work, *Imperialism: The Highest Stage of Capitalism*.) It was

social organization. He had supplanted dialectic materialism with progressive idealism. He had destroyed both the necessity and the possibility of revolution, and had raised political and social reform from the level of means to the level of ends." See also Peter Gay, *The Dilemma of Democratic Socialism: Eduard Bernstein's Challenge to Marx* (New York: Columbia University Press, 1952), esp. Chaps. 7-8.

22. Kautsky, quoted in Schorske, *German Social Democracy*, pp. 111-115.

Kautsky's opinion that imperialism did *not* serve the interests of modern capitalism. Through the immense costs of the arms race it had engendered, it was interfering with capital accumulation. Rival nation-states, therefore, would need to reach mutual agreements to reduce the economic burdens of armaments. It was even conceivable to Kautsky that a further stage of capitalist development (which he called "ultra-imperialism") might witness the peaceable organization of the world economy. International conflict among the imperialist powers, according to Kautsky's analysis, was neither politically nor economically necessary.[23]

Cf. Mandel

Thus revisionist Marxists of the early twentieth century disagreed fundamentally with Marxist-Leninists on a number of basic issues. What is more, these disagreements have endured to the present. Contemporary Social Democrats have little tolerance for or interest in traditional Marxist notions of revolution. Such socialists employ a class analysis but, unlike "orthodox" Marxists, question the revolutionary character of the working class. So also do they reject the Communist belief in certain inexorable laws of history that guarantee the eventual triumph of the proletarian cause. The future, for them, remains open and undetermined, not certain and predetermined. Nor are they absolutely confident that a maturing capitalism *inevitably* produces international conflict. That, too, remains an open question. Yet there is in Social Democratic theory a clear recognition that the institutions and representatives of corporate capital—both financial and industrial—represent a pernicious and powerful influence. It is far more likely under capitalism than under socialism that leading economic interests will have the need and ability to persuade decision-makers to engage in imperialist aggression and war.[24]

23. Schorske, *German Social Democracy*, pp. 244-246. See also Karl Kautsky, "Ultra-imperialism," an article completed several weeks before the outbreak of World War I and reprinted in *New Left Review*, 59 (January-February 1970), pp. 41-46.

24. On revisionist socialism see, among others, George Lichtheim, *Marxism in Modern France* (New York: Columbia University Press, 1966);

A comprehensive delineation of the revisionist Marxist explanation of contemporary imperialism and war is rendered difficult by the paucity of Social Democratic theorizing since Kautsky. This virtual theoretical void is surprising, considering the political successes of democratic socialism in Western Europe. Nonetheless, the basic contours of such an explanation may be discerned from the writings of the prolific philosopher and social critic, George Lichtheim (1912-1973).

Joining earlier revisionists in his unwillingness to identify Marxism with Leninism and in his belief that the "prospects for socialism are brightest where economic pressures are negligible," Lichtheim scorned Marxist-Leninists and liberals alike. His social-democratic variant of Marxist theory provided a harsh critique of the alleged rigidity of Soviet Marxism. For Lichtheim, Marxism was to be treated as a method of analysis, not as a set of incontrovertible propositions about the world.

In an extended essay on imperialism published in 1971, Lichtheim firmly rejected Leninist notions regarding the exploitative character of imperialist investments and their retarding impact on Third World development. He was equally impatient with Maoist "deviations" from Marx that in his view incorrectly equate nationalism with socialism, the peasantry with the proletariat, populism with Marxism. From his perspective, it is absurd to argue that nationalist revolutionary movements of the Vietnamese type can defeat either capitalism or imperialism as a world system.[25]

In an even more recent work, written shortly before his

---

and David Coates, *The Labour Party and the Struggle for Socialism* (London: Cambridge University Press, 1975).

25. See Lichtheim, *Imperialism* (New York: Frederick A. Praeger, 1971), pp. 115, 141-150. But on pp. 165-166 he makes a statement that appears to contradict his position stated above: "The real question is not whether capitalism exploits the underdeveloped countries—of course it does, and always has—but why it has not done more to revolutionize them through the very mechanism of exploitation."

death, Lichtheim summarized his position regarding imperialism and war:

If the international system breaks down, it will not be due to the automatism of rival economic systems, but to incompatible political ambitions on the part of the nuclear super-powers. The stakes have grown too high for commercial rivalry to play the role it did in 1914, and still to some extent in 1939. Nor is the East-West antagonism reducible to a conflict between capitalist and socialist system. In short, the Leninist perspective of the 1920s has ceased to apply. Were it otherwise, there ought to be a Leninist explanation for the growing enmity between Russia and China. The fact that there is none demonstrates that the age of economic rivalry giving rise to political conflict has been left behind.[26]

Lichtheim's recognition of the political factor does not constitute an abandonment of his basic Marxist perspective, but it does indicate the continuing divergence in the theoretical analyses of Marxist-Leninists and Social Democratic Marxists.[27]

26. Lichtheim, *Europe in the Twentieth Century* (New York: Frederick A. Praeger, 1972), p. 304.

27. Beginning in the 1960s and continuing in the 1970s, a highly diverse group of "New Left" scholars, largely American, advanced what has often been viewed as a radical interpretation of corporate capitalism and American foreign policy. Some representatives of this "school"—William Appleman Williams, Walter LaFeber, and Gabriel Kolko, for example—move reasonably close to an orthodox Marxist position by accounting for the rise of an expansionist American empire in terms of a search for overseas raw materials, markets, and foreign trade. They also stress the calculated use of political means by corporate elites to achieve economic penetration of Third World regions. In general, however, despite great interest in the origins of the Cold War and the Vietnam conflict, New Left scholars lack a systematic theory of war.

One of the problems in dealing with this group of scholars is that the "New Left" category is used as a kind of interpretive dumping ground for all those of revisionist and critical persuasion. We badly need a careful critique of these New Left scholars designed to probe their ideological and theoretical assumptions. For general discussions, see, among others: Carl Ogelsby (ed.), *The New Left Reader* (New York: Grove Press, 1969); Lyman Tower Sargent, *New Left Thought: An Introduction* (Homewood, Ill.: Dorsey, 1972); and Irwin Unger, *The Movement: A History of the American New Left* (New York: Dodd, Mead, 1974). For an essay that points to the essential liberalism of several New Left students of American foreign policy, see Lloyd E. Ambrosius, "The Orthodoxy of Revisionism: Woodrow Wilson and the New Left," *Diplomatic History*, 1 (Summer 1977), pp. 199-214.

Also representative of this divergence is the contribution of a group of European peace researchers whose foremost practitioner is the Norwegian Johan Galtung (1930-   ). In a manner similar to the Maoists, but without their commitment to orthodox Marxism, Galtung and his colleagues are exploring the North-South, more than the East-West, dimension of international relations. Galtung, for example, has developed a "structural" theory of imperialism that seeks to explain the relationship between rich (or "topdog") nation-states and poor (or "underdog") ones. Like other scholars of Marxist and near-Marxist persuasion, Galtung argues that the rich control and exploit the poor on an international level through trade, investment, and the operations of multinational corporations. Thus for him it is no surprise when asymmetrical (underdog-topdog) conflict breaks out, or even when certain forms of symmetrical (underdog-underdog) conflict occur. For topdog-topdog conflict, however, his explanations are not so largely grounded in economics, involving, aside from material factors, aggression by states that do not have the status recognition to which they are entitled.[28]

CONCLUSION

Our examination of the major radical theories of war has revealed a wide variety of interpretations of social reality deriving from the Marxist perspective. Such a diversity of explanations flowing from a single theoretical source leads one to wonder whether Marxism has come to mean what-

28. See Johan Galtung, "A Structural Theory of Aggression," *Journal of Peace Research*, 1 (1964), pp. 95-119; Galtung, "A Structural Theory of Imperialism," *Journal of Peace Research*, 8 (1971), pp. 81-117; Galtung, "Peace Thinking," in Albert Lepawsky, Edward H. Buehrig, and Harold D. Lasswell (eds.), *The Search for World Order* (New York: Appleton-Century-Crofts, 1971), pp. 120-153; Kenneth N. Waltz, "Theory of International Relations," in Fred I. Greenstein and Nelson W. Polsby (eds.), *International Politics* (Reading, Mass.: Addison-Wesley, 1975), pp. 26-33; and Jagdish N. Bhagwati (ed.), *The New International Order: The North-South Debate* (Cambridge, Mass.: M.I.T. Press, 1977).

ever Marxists choose it to mean. Indeed, radicals have not only disagreed about the use of their own theory, but have often done so with fervent intensity. We have noted, for example, the severe reaction by "orthodox," revolutionary Marxists of the early twentieth century to the gradualist, evolutionary "heresy" of the "revisionist" Social Democrats.

Nevertheless, while we acknowledge the rich diversity of radical thought and the often bitter struggles waged on the Left, we also stress the manner in which the ideological assumptions of radicalism permeate *all* radical theories of war. Radicalism, as was suggested earlier in this chapter, draws inspiration from a variety of sources, but its primary wellspring is Marxism. And, like Karl Marx, radicals—whether Leninist, Maoist, or Social Democrat—locate the causes of war in capitalist economic institutions and emphasize the connection between domestic structures and international conflict. Furthermore, radical theorists generally explain war as being the consequence of rational and premeditated (not irrational or accidental) decisions of a ruling class or ruling groups. In the sphere of war, then, human actors have limited choice, because long-term, structural factors are governing.

CHAPTER FOUR

Historians and World War I

THE EXISTING INTERPRETIVE FRAMEWORK

In order to demonstrate the usefulness of the categorizations we have devised for analyzing studies of war, it is necessary for us to relate them to a significant number of interpretations of a significant number of major conflicts. Only in this way can we show that, in fact, (1) ideology does influence theory, (2) historians do have ideologies as well as theories which correspond to our major ideal types but about which they are not always conscious or consistent, and (3) we can better understand, compare, and evaluate what historians are saying when we comprehend their ideological and theoretical perspectives. We can also cast new light on longstanding historiographical controversies, revealing to what extent their noise and thunder may disguise basic agreements or disagreements about assumptions or crucial data.

To accomplish our objective we have chosen to examine writings about two great twentieth-century conflicts: World War I and World War II. We have selected these conflicts not on any random basis but because they are obviously important, complex, and well documented. They also have in common certain social, political, and technological characteristics (for example, that their belligerents possessed such constituent elements as cities, political parties, and sophisticated communications media) the absence of which might make comparisons of their histories much more difficult. We do believe, however, that the categories we offer can be utilized to assist in mastering the historiography of any war or comparable phenomenon (see the Epilogue).

To set the scene for scrutinizing the several interpretations of World War I we must briefly trace the course of the historical debate about that subject. This will enable the reader to put each of the historians and his commentary within an essentially familiar context. It will also allow one to compare and contrast the traditional view of the writing in question with our own.

To be sure, to survey the historiography of World War I is no easy task. Seldom has as much been written about any historical topic. Seldom have attitudes and beliefs regarding the causation of an event changed as rapidly or as continually as with that war; hardly a decade has passed that has not witnessed a significant shift in the dominant interpretation.

There were plenty of grounds for disagreement from the beginning, of course. Not only did the partisans of the belligerent powers dispute most bitterly about the leaders and the peoples who were responsible for the great catastrophe, but within each nation there was also an alienated (and largely unheard) minority which upheld a view or views at odds with that of the controlling majority. In a very real sense all of the interpretations which historians have offered since the war were foreshadowed by explanations developed by participants at the time. And since the three ideological traditions which we have identified were present, to a greater or lesser extent, in each of the warring countries, this fact should perhaps occasion no great surprise.

Still, the vast majority of the Allied (and especially the American) peoples quickly accepted the notion that Germany and Austria-Hungary had initiated hostilities, and held fast to this idea for several years after the conflict. The hysteria and hatred of the war era were such that few found cause to quarrel with the conclusions of the study commission of the Paris Peace Conference (1919) that "the war was premeditated by the Central Powers . . . , and was the result of acts deliberately committed in order to make it unavoidable."[1] As late as 1922 there were relatively few Allied misgivings about the fact that Germany had been forced in Article 231 of the Treaty of Versailles to accept responsibility for the loss and damage suffered in consequence of a "war imposed by the aggression of Germany and her allies."[2]

Gradually, however, as wartime passions ebbed and as the defeated nations began to open their archives in the attempt to exonerate themselves, the perspectives of the victors changed. Working from Austrian and German documents, the historian Sidney Fay was able to demonstrate even in 1920 and 1921 that Vienna's policy of 1914 was not dictated by Berlin and that the civilian leaders in both Russia and Germany had been misled by their respective militaries.[3] Later in the 1920s, as "revisionism" gained wider and wider acceptance, Fay attempted to "put on the brakes" by emphasizing the extent of German diplomatic stupidity, and his magnum opus *The Origins of the World War* (1928) made it clear that, in his view, the preponderance of guilt remained with the Central Powers.[4] Yet by 1928 the revisionists were largely winning the battle for the popular mind. Writers like Maximilian Montgelas (*The Case for the Central Powers*, 1923), Harry Elmer Barnes (*The Genesis of the World War*, 1926), and Hermann Lutz (*Lord Grey and the World War*, 1927) had done much to persuade the Allied publics not only

1. From the Carnegie Endowment, *German White Book Concerning the Responsibility of the Authors of the War* (New York: Oxford University Press, 1924), p. 21.
2. Philip Mason Burnett, *Reparation at the Paris Peace Conference*, 2 vols. (New York: Columbia University Press, 1940), Vol. I, p. 142.
3. Sidney B. Fay, "New Light on the Origins of the World War," *American Historical Review*, 25 (July 1920) pp. 616-639, 26 (October 1920 and January 1921) pp. 37-53, 225-254.
4. Selig Adler, "The War Guilt Question and American Disillusionment, 1918-1928," *Journal of Modern History*, 23 (March 1951), p. 11; Sidney B. Fay, *The Origins of the World War* (New York: Macmillan, 1928).

that all powers shared the responsibility for the war but also that France and Russia had been particularly aggressive.[5] The studies of more orthodox scholars such as Pierre Renouvin (*Immediate Origins of the War*, 1925) and Bernadotte Schmitt (*The Coming of the War 1914*, 1930) were only marginally successful in stemming the tide.[6] Schmitt might argue persuasively that "no diplomacy, however skillful, could have devised a compromise between the firm resolutions of Austrian-Hungary to make war on Serbia and the determination of Russia not to permit the crushing of that small state,"[7] but Barnes was more representative of the mood of the day in contending that whatever the Dual Monarchy had done was done only in the interest of self-preservation and that if Germany had really wanted a war, she would have fought long before 1914.

Under the impact of the Great Depression, disillusionment with the Allied cause grew even more pronounced and explanations often assumed a more radical tone. No longer were historians content simply to rank the belligerent countries in the order of their alleged guilt; now attention was commonly focused on social, economic, and institutional questions having to do with a nation's policies. In the isolationist United States, where debate centered on the reasons why America had become involved in the conflict, authors like Walter Millis (*Road to War*, 1935), C. Hartley Grattan (*Preface to Chaos,* 1936), and Charles Beard (*The*

5. Maximilian Montgelas, *The Case for the Central Powers* (New York: Alfred A. Knopf, 1925; published in German in 1923); Harry Elmer Barnes, *The Genesis of the World War* (New York: Alfred A. Knopf, 1926); Hermann Lutz, *Lord Grey and the World War* (New York: Alfred A. Knopf, 1928; published in German in 1927). See also Maximilian Montgelas, *British Foreign Policy under Sir Edward Grey* (New York: Alfred A. Knopf, 1928), and Alfred von Wegerer, *Refutation of the Versailles War Guilt Thesis* (New York: Alfred A. Knopf, 1930).

6. Pierre Renouvin, *The Immediate Origins of the War* (New Haven: Yale University Press, 1928; published in French in 1927); Bernadotte E. Schmitt, *The Coming of the War 1914*, 2 vols. (New York: Charles Scribner's Sons, 1930).

7. Schmitt, *The Coming of the War 1914*, Vol. 2, p. 480.

Devil Theory of War, 1936) pointed out the extent to which President Wilson had been the victim in 1917 of such forces as Allied propaganda and American economic involvement in Britain and France.[8] On the European side analogous perspectives were developed regarding their own countries by Eckart Kehr (*Schlachtflottenbau und Parteipolitik*, 1930) and Georges Michon (*La Préparation à la guerre*, 1935).[9] Even more critical of capitalism was Konni Zilliacus (*Mirror of the Past*, 1946).[10]

The experience of World War II understandably tended to drive historians back in the direction of assigning a major responsibility for the earlier war to the Germans. On occasion what emerged was a rather severe indictment, as with Luigi Albertini's classic three-volume study (*The Origins of the War of 1914*, 1942), which puts the primary blame upon the German military caste and "its utter lack of political horse sense."[11] More generally the picture that developed was less one-sided, with Germany only the most clumsy of the many nations which (in David Lloyd George's famous phrase) had "stumbled into war." A. J. P. Taylor (*The*

8. Walter Millis, *Road to War: America, 1914-1917* (New York: Houghton Mifflin, 1935); C. Hartley Grattan, *Preface to Chaos: War in the Making* (New York: Dodge, 1936); Charles A. Beard, *The Devil Theory of War* (New York: Vanguard Press, 1936). See also Warren I. Cohen, *The American Revisionists: The Lessons of Intervention in World War I* (Chicago: University of Chicago Press, 1967).

9. Eckart Kehr, *Schlachtflottenbau und Parteipolitik 1894-1901* (Berlin: E. Ebering, 1930); Georges Michon, *La Préparation à la guerre: La loi des trois ans (1910-1914)* (Paris: M. Rivere, 1935). See also Georg W. F. Hallgarten, *Imperialismus vor 1914: Die Soziologischen Grundlagen der Aussenpolitik europäischer Grossmächte vor dem ersten Weltkrieg*, 2 vols., 2nd edition (Munich: C. H. Beck, 1961; manuscript completed in 1933).

10. Konni Zilliacus, *Mirror of the Past: A History of Secret Diplomacy* (New York: Current Books, 1946).

11. Luigi Albertini, *The Origins of the War of 1914*, 3 vols. (Oxford: Oxford University Press, 1957; published in Italian in 1942), Vol. III, p. 253. Such an "orthodox" position had been ably defended during the 1930s, with regard to United States involvement in the war, by Charles Seymour. See his *American Diplomacy During the World War* (Hamden, Conn.: Archon, 1934) and *American Neutrality, 1914-1917* (Hamden, Conn.: Archon, 1935).

Struggle for Mastery in Europe, 1954), after emphasizing that the Germans had decided in 1914 "to use their superior powers either to win a war or to achieve a striking success," went on to concede that all European statesmen "were inclined to think that war would stave off their social and political problems."[12] Raymond Aron (*The Century of Total War*, 1954) asserted that there was no inevitable trend of events toward war but simply a series of acts by sovereign states seeking what seemed to them at the time to be their own best interests.[13] A conference of Franco-German historians in 1951 concluded that "the documents do not allow one to ascribe in 1914 to any one government or people the conscious desire for a European war."[14]

Despite this apparent consensus, however, only a few years were to pass before a new and bitter debate had developed with regard to the origins of World War I. In 1959 the German historian Fritz Fischer began publishing a series of writings (*Germany's Aims in the First World War*, 1961; *War of Illusions*, 1969) which ultimately put forward the startling thesis that the German Empire had not only desired and prepared for war but consciously provoked it.[15] Fischer's studies were very much in accord with the anti-

12. A. J. P. Taylor, *The Struggle for Mastery in Europe 1848-1918* (Oxford: Clarendon Press, 1954), pp. 522-529.

13. Raymond Aron, *The Century of Total War* (Garden City, N.Y.: Doubleday, 1954), p. 13. This was somewhat similar to the view of American "Realist" historians, who, with regard to the events of 1917, were intensely critical of Wilsonian moralism but not of American participation in maintaining the balance of power. See, for example, Walter Lippmann, *U.S. Foreign Policy: Shield of the Republic* (Boston: Little, Brown, 1943); George F. Kennan, *American Diplomacy, 1900-1950* (Chicago: University of Chicago Press, 1951); and Robert E. Osgood, *Ideals and Self-Interest in America's Foreign Relations: The Great Transformation of the Twentieth Century* (Chicago: University of Chicago Press, 1953).

14. The agreement was published by Gerhard Ritter as "Vereinbarung der deutschen und französischen Historiker," *Die Welt als Geschichte*, 12 (1952), pp. 145-148.

15. Fritz Fischer, *Germany's Aims in the First World War* (New York: W. W. Norton, 1967; published in German in 1961); Fischer, *War of Illusions: German Policies from 1911 to 1914* (London: Chatto and Windus, 1975; published in German in 1969).

establishment mood of the 1960s, but he did not lack critics, especially in Germany, where for four decades the assertion of German innocence in 1914 had been almost an article of faith for all parties. By early 1962 the "Fischer controversy" had enveloped the German historical profession as the accuser was in turn accused of misjudgment by a variety of older scholars.[16] The best known of his attackers was Gerhard Ritter, the recognized dean of German historians and the author himself of a four-volume study of modern militarism, *The Sword and the Scepter* (1954-1968).[17] Ritter and others like Hans Herzfeld and Karl Dietrich Erdmann sprang in particular to the defense of Chancellor Theobald von Bethmann-Hollweg, contending that the German leader's policy had been basically pacific and that the only real problem had been in the subordination of the political establishment to the military caste.[18]

Waged vigorously during the middle 1960s, this historiographical conflict was supplemented and supplanted toward the end of the decade by the onslaught of younger and more radical German historians. Hans-Ulrich Wehler (*Das Deutsche Kaiserreich*, 1973) emerged as the spokesman of this school, which, like its inspiration Eckart Kehr, was dedicated to putting the socio-economic and other structural elements at the heart of the historical enterprise.[19]

16. See Wolfgang J. Mommsen, "The Debate on German War Aims," *Journal of Contemporary History*, 1 (July 1966), pp. 45-70; James Joll, "The 1914 Debate Continues: Fritz Fischer and His Critics," *Past and Present*, No. 34 (July 1966), pp. 100-113; and Immanuel Geiss (ed.), *July 1914; The Outbreak of the First World War: Selected Documents* (New York: W. W. Norton, 1967), pp. 9-16.

17. Gerhard Ritter, *The Sword and the Scepter: The Problem of Militarism in Germany*, 4 vols. (Coral Gables, Fla.: University of Miami Press, 1969-1972; published in German, 1954-1968).

18. Hans Herzfeld, "Die deutsche Kriegspolitik im Ersten Weltkrieg," *Vierteljahrshefte für Zeitgeschichte*, 11 (July 1963), pp. 224-245; Karl Dietrich Erdmann, "Zur Beurteilung Bethmann-Hollwegs," *Geschichte in Wissenschaft und Unterricht*, 15 (September 1964), pp. 525-540. For a useful collection of the most substantial articles in the controversy, see Wolfgang Schieder (ed.), *Erster Weltkrieg: Uraschen, Enstehung und Kriegsziele* (Cologne: Kiepenheuer & Witsch, 1969).

19. See Hans-Ulrich Wehler, *Bismarck und der Imperialismus* (Co-

Other representatives of the "Kehr-ite" approach included Dirk Stegmann (*Die Erben Bismarcks*, 1970) and Volker Berghahn (*Germany and the Approach of War in 1914*, 1973).[20] These authors argued that the politics of imperialism and navalism in Germany had been the means by which the middle and upper classes had united and maintained their privileged positions against the socialists. What had finally happened, they said, was that "the country's ruling elites [became so] . . . haunted by the nightmare of impending internal chaos and external defeat . . . that an offensive war appeared to be the only way out."[21]

Historians outside of West Germany also participated in the trends and tendencies of the 1960s and 1970s. In East Germany a small but increasingly respected group of scholars including Fritz Klein (*Deutschland im ersten Weltkrieg*, 1968) and Willibald Gutsche was even more eager than the Wehler school to attribute responsibility for the war to the "contradictions inherent in capitalism."[22] In the United States, on the other hand, the dominant voices were somewhat more cautious than in West Germany. In the early 1960s American social scientists such as Bruce Russett, Robert North, and Ole Holsti developed a considerable interest in the causes of World War I but approached it consistently from the standpoint that both sides in the dispute

logne: Kiepenheuer & Witsch, 1969); Wehler, *Das Deutsche Kaiserreich 1871-1918* (Göttingen: Vandenhoeck & Ruprecht, 1973). See also Wolfgang J. Mommsen, "Domestic Factors in German Foreign Policy before 1914," *Central European History*, 6 (March 1973), pp. 8-16; and Georg G. Iggers, *New Directions in European Historiography* (Middletown, Conn.: Wesleyan University Press, 1975), pp. 102-112.

20. Dirk Stegmann, *Die Erben Bismarcks* (Cologne: Kiepenheuer & Witsch, 1970); Volker Berghahn, *Germany and the Approach of War in 1914* (New York: St. Martin's Press, 1973).

21. Berghahn, *Germany and the Approach of War in 1914*, p. 213.

22. Fritz Klein *et al., Deutschland im ersten Weltkrieg, I: Vorbereitung, Entfesslung und Verlauf des Krieges bis Ende 1914* (Berlin: Akademie Verlag, 1968); Willibald Gutsche, *Aufstieg und Fall eines kaiserlichen Reichskanzlers: Theobald von Bethmann-Hollweg 1856-1921* (Berlin: Akademie Verlag, 1973).

had made the same kind of contributions to its escalation.[23] Later, as the Fischer controversy broke over Germany, some Americans like Hajo Holborn welcomed a harsher view of Wilhelminian policy, seeing in it a confirmation of the work of Schmitt, Renouvin, and Albertini.[24] Still later, in the tide of the Vietnam War, such observers as Arno Mayer (*Dynamics of Counterrevolution in Europe, 1870-1956*, 1971) were obviously responding to the same currents that had touched Wehler and Berghahn in Europe.[25]

By the middle 1970s an element of moderation and orthodoxy had returned. Scholars like Oron J. Hale (*The Great Illusion, 1900-1914*, 1971) and Konrad Jarausch (*The Enigmatic Chancellor*, 1973) were not afraid to put the spotlight once again upon the personality of participants; nor were they hesitant about placing the largest responsibility for the war upon the leadership of the Central Powers.[26] Yet in their work and the writings of such individuals as Fritz Stern

23. Bruce Russett, "Cause, Surprise, and No Escape," *The Journal of Politics*, 24 (February 1962), pp. 3-22; Ole Holsti and Robert C. North, "Perceptions of Hostility and Economic Variables," in Richard L. Merritt (ed.), *Comparing Nations* (New Haven: Yale University Press, 1965); Ole Holsti, "The 1914 Case," *American Political Science Review*, 59 (June 1965), pp. 365-378. See also Eugenie V. Nomikos and Robert C. North, *International Crisis: The Outbreak of World War I* (Montreal: McGill-Queens University Press, 1976). During the late 1950s and early 1960s historians of American involvement in World War I were every bit as cautious as the social scientists, emphasizing complexity, inevitability, and heroism in the face of necessity. See Arthur S. Link, *Wilson the Diplomatist: A Look at His Major Foreign Polices* (Baltimore: Johns Hopkins 1957), and Ernest R. May, *The World War and American Isolation, 1914-1917* (Cambridge, Mass.: Harvard University Press, 1959).

24. See Hajo Holborn's introduction to Fritz Fischer, *Germany's Aims in the First World War* (American edition, 1967) pp. x-xi.

25. Arno Mayer, *Dynamics of Counterrevolution in Europe, 1870-1956: An Analytic Framework* (New York: Harper and Row, 1971). For a comparable point of view regarding American involvement, see N. Gordon Levin, *Woodrow Wilson and World Politics: America's Response to War and Revolution* (New York: Oxford University Press, 1968).

26. Oron J. Hale, *The Great Illusion, 1900-1914* (New York: Harper and Row, 1971); Konrad H. Jarausch, *The Enigmatic Chancellor: Bethmann-Hollweg and the Hubris of Imperial Germany* (New Haven: Yale University Press, 1973).

(*The Failure of Illiberalism*, 1972) and Michael Gordon ("Domestic Conflict and the Origins of the First World War," 1974) one gets a sense of historical and social context that enables one to be relatively nonjudgmental.[27] More often than not, and particularly in later years, historians of World War I had called attention to the causal importance of such "non-immediate" factors as alliance systems, the arms race, superheated nationalisms, and lack of democratic governments. Now, however, there was a somewhat greater tendency, perhaps derived from the insights of the 1960s, to put these factors into a dynamic and coherent structure of interrelated parts: social, economic, political, and psychological.

A NEW INTERPRETIVE FRAMEWORK

It is in the face of such growing self-consciousness and coherence as well as the apparently overwhelming diversity of historical interpretation that the authors of this volume turn to a new and more systematic framework for evaluation. It is not our intention, of course, to apply our approach to every one or even the majority of the scholars whose names have been mentioned above. Rather, we wish to show by a careful examination of a few individuals that this kind of analysis can be helpful whenever it is used, often revealing differences and similarities where they are not expected. In this instance we shall focus on the following historians: as examples of the conservative perspective, Edmund Stillman and William Pfaff;[28] as examples of lib-

27. Fritz Stern, *The Failure of Illiberalism: Essays on the Political Culture of Modern Germany* (New York: Alfred A. Knopf, 1972); Michael Gordon, "Domestic Conflict and the Origins of the First World War: The British and German Cases," *Journal of Modern History*, 46 (June 1974), pp. 191-266. See also Jonathan Steinberg, "The Armistice in German History," *Times Literary Supplement*, October 25, 1974.

28. See Edmund Stillman and William Pfaff, *The Politics of Hysteria: The Sources of Twentieth Century Conflict* (New York: Harper and Row, 1964).

eral points of view, Sidney B. Fay, Ole Holsti, G. Lowes Dickinson, Fritz Fischer, and Gerhard Ritter; as examples of radical commentary, Fritz Klein and Konni Zilliacus.

The Conservative Tradition and World War I Historiography: Edmund Stillman and William Pfaff

Though World War I engendered profound disillusionment and cultural pessimism, traits closely related to those of conservative temperament, it is a surprising fact that the conservative perspective is not well represented among historians of that conflict. Rather, the scholarly battle with regard to 1914 has been waged largely among individuals of liberal persuasion. Apparently both the era since the war and the academic establishment have been far too liberal for conservatism (and radicalism) to show up other than among "outsider" intellectuals.

To be sure, on occasion the outsider to the academy could be one of the participating "insiders" of the government. Thus, Winston Churchill, First Lord of the Admiralty when war broke out and later Minister of Munitions in Lloyd George's coalition, published five volumes on *The World Crisis* which offer a largely conservative interpretation.[29] "One rises from the study of the causes of the Great War," he wrote, "with a prevailing sense of the defective control of individuals upon world fortunes."[30] Yet even Churchill, the scion of an aristocratic family and ultimately Britain's greatest Tory, was not thoroughly and consistently conservative. He might assert that "the story of the human race is War,"[31] but the reader looks in vain for an accusation against the people at large or for a demand that authority be rendered more hierarchical. And though Churchill spoke of "fierce resentments" existing among the French and Russians,[32] he was also willing to describe Germany as "[clanking] ob-

29. Winston S. Churchill, *The World Crisis*, 5 vols. (New York: Charles Scribner's Sons, 1927-1930).
30. Churchill, *The World Crisis*, I, p. 13.
31. Churchill, *The World Crisis*, V, p. 479.
32. Churchill, *The World Crisis*, I, p. 14.

stinately, recklessly, awkwardly toward the crater and [dragging] us all in."[33]

A somewhat "purer" example of conservative interpretation was produced in the 1960s by two Americans who also stood somewhat outside the main historiographical tradition: Edmund Stillman and William Pfaff. *The Politics of Hysteria* (1964) was the second of three collaborative works on public affairs written by Stillman and Pfaff, the others being *The New Politics* (1961), and *Power and Impotence* (1966). Stillman has also edited *Bitter Harvest: The Intellectual Revolt Behind the Iron Curtain* (1959). Pfaff has published a volume about the modern predicament entitled *Condemned to Freedom* (1971).

The authors came to their study from diverse backgrounds. Edmund Stillman, born in 1924, received a B.A. degree in English from Yale University in 1945 and an L.L.B. from Columbia University Law School in 1947. A Foreign Service Officer for the Department of State from 1947 to 1951, he later conducted strategic research for several private American organizations. A longtime member of the Hudson Institute, Stillman has also participated in study groups for the Council of Foreign Relations and, during 1962-1963, served as a research fellow of the Russian Institute of Columbia University. He is a member of the New York Bar.

William Pfaff was born in Iowa in 1928 and attended public and parochial schools there and in Georgia. Graduated from the University of Notre Dame in 1949, in subsequent years he became an editor and correspondent for *Commonweal* and an executive of the Free Europe Committee. He joined the Hudson Institute in 1961, later taking a year's leave to serve as a research fellow for the Columbia University Russian Institute.[34]

In *The Politics of Hysteria* Stillman and Pfaff are at-

33. *Ibid.*, p. 13.
34. The biographical information is from Stillman and Pfaff, *The Politics of Hysteria*, pp. 275-276; and William Pfaff, *Condemned to Freedom* (New York: Random House, 1971), p. 211.

tempting "to describe the quality of political action and to explore the relationship between that action and the past of modern culture and society."[35] They begin by attacking the optimism and complacent rationalism of the political doctrines we have inherited from another age and which take no account of "the intimidating lessons of the first half of our century—the renewed evidence of the irrational and truly demonic in man."[36] There is need, they assert, for an attitude of prudence—an attitude whose essence "lies not with exorcising ambition, but in moderating it and bending it in politics to finite ends."[37] "History is 'made' only in the sense that men's efforts to 'make' history—to practice politics—inevitably produce a result which surprises their intentions."[38]

It is thus the politics of optimism, or as Stillman and Pfaff call it, "the politics of hysteria," which poses the greatest danger to our survival. It is Western man's naive belief in universal formulations—"innocent, stripped of humanity, stripped of a consciousness of tragedy, of historical predicament, of irrationality, of perversity and malice in ignorant and sinful men"[39]—which may ultimately lead him into despair or into the self-destruction of "magical totalitarianism." "It comes down to this," assert the authors, "if we would survive, we must draw back. In the old words of Talleyrand, the condition of modern survival is not merely wisdom and strength, but 'pas trop de zèle'—above all, not too much zeal."[40]

World War I is suggested by Stillman and Pfaff as an example not only of the perversity of the species but also of the overzealousness of modern man.

No single cause will explain the First World War. But the formal causes—the commercial and colonial rivalries, the cocked war establishments of Europe designed to mobilize, deploy, and conquer by the execution of a single and irreversible general-staff plan,

35. Stillman and Pfaff, *The Politics of Hysteria*, p. 1.
36. *Ibid.*, p. 7.   37. *Ibid.*, p. 252.   38. *Ibid.*, p. 251.
39. *Ibid.*, p. 246   40. *Ibid.*, p. 254.

the strident minorities and grandiose nationalisms, the disintegration of the Austro-Hungarian Europe, the colonial rivalries, the rot of Turkey, the instability of the balance of power—all these pale before the fact that Europe in 1914 wanted war and got it.[41]

Or again:

It is impossible to reflect upon the immense tragedy of the First World War without realizing that the Western nations which waged it were driven by something very near to a pathological will to self-destruction.[42]

And finally:

What was in the air by 1914 was a spirit of violent repudiation of the age that can scarcely be accounted for in any objective historical or political terms, but only by a judgment on human character. The nineteenth century had abolished war; but the peace and stability of that world perished because men could hardly bear to live for a century with the kind of world they had made.[43]

What Stillman and Pfaff offer us, therefore, is an interesting and subtle variation on an old conservative theme. This is quite obviously not a simple-minded assertion that men and nations treat each other like animals and that life is a constant war of all against all. Neither is it a brief on behalf of an existing aristocracy or a particular balance of power. Elites and peoples seem equally corruptible;[44] power as such is hardly mentioned except in reference to the triumph of the "modern" West over the "traditional" East.[45] Nevertheless, when all is done, the validity of a Burkean analysis is accepted at almost every turn. As William Pfaff puts it in his later book: "Depersonalization, dissolution of social bonds, dissociation of individuals from tradition and community, secularization, the idolatry of science, the abusive centralization of power: we might as well be recounting . . . the established European conservative's critique, even the reactionary's attack upon the modern liberal world."[46] These are the factors and developments, then, that Stillman and Pfaff

41. *Ibid.*, p. 117.   42. *Ibid.*, p. 120.   43. *Ibid.*, p. 111.
44. See, for example, *ibid.*, p. 245.   45. See *ibid.*, pp. 37-54.
46. Pfaff, *Condemned to Freedom*, p. 125.

believe were responsible for the mood which proved to be so destructive in 1914. In their view, the process of modernization had irreversibly undermined our psychic stability, operating on an earlier generation just as they see it continuing to operate in the present day. "Condemned to be free," Western man lives in an age of conservative needs in which conservative solutions are no longer entirely possible. The best we can do is to grope forward with patience and humility, striving honestly for a greater sharing of community and more humane relationships. Only by lowering expectations without at the same time abandoning hope and idealism will it be possible for us to improve the quality of life and to avoid the recurrence of such tragic disasters as that which began in 1914.

The Liberal Tradition and World War I Historiography: Sidney B. Fay, Ole Holsti, G. Lowes Dickinson, Fritz Fischer, and Gerhard Ritter

To repeat, in moving from the conservative to the liberal historical realm, we find that the latter is much better supplied with interpretations of 1914 than was the former. Indeed, it would not be too much to say that the liberals have dominated the historiography of World War I from the beginning. Within and along the boundaries of their three major paradigms, liberal historians have offered us much imaginative and thoughtful history, as well as some that is relatively jumbled.

The Social-Psychological Interpretation: Sidney B. Fay and Ole Holsti. The social-psychological view of World War I, though often somewhat disguised in presentation, has long been well represented among historians. For our purposes it will suffice to scrutinize two examples of this perspective—the one a classic history of the subject, the other a recent attempt to amass data at certain crucial historical points. The first, by Sidney B. Fay (1876-1967), is perhaps the most substantial work produced by a scholar in the 1920s about the causes of the war. The second, by Ole

Holsti (1933-), is in the form of several essays and a relatively brief and quite narrow book. Nevertheless, whereas Fay's historical theory is diffuse and implicit, Holsti's by comparison is clear-cut and explicit.

Sidney Fay's *The Origins of the World War*, as we noted earlier, was not published until eight years after his "New Light" articles had attracted so much attention. The book had been awaited by revisionists and anti-revisionists alike, since Fay was universally respected, but when it finally appeared its evenhandedness was a great disappointment to both camps.[47] Nonetheless, *Origins* won Fay a professorship at Harvard, where he had earned both his B.A. (1896) and Ph.D. (1900) and where he now returned to teach from 1929 to 1946. Specializing in German history, Fay published *The Rise of Brandenburg Prussia* in 1937 and a number of related articles in succeeding years. In 1946 he climaxed his career by serving as president of the American Historical Association.

Fay begins the argument of *Origins* by recognizing the distinction originally made by Thucydides between the more remote, or underlying, causes of war and those that are more immediate. The former he describes as the "inflammable material which has been heaped up through the long period of years"; the latter as "the final spark which starts the conflagration." Emphasizing that "responsibility for the underlying causes does not always coincide with responsibility for the immediate causes," Fay goes on to identify a number of underlying causes for which all the major European powers were "more or less responsible." Among these he includes (1) "the system of secret alliances which developed in Europe after the Franco-Prussian War" and which was "the greatest single underlying cause" of the later conflict; (2) "the system of great armies," with its attendant body of war-minded military and naval officers, its secret

47. Adler, "The War Guilt Question and American Disillusionment," pp. 23-24.

military plans, and its pressure from munitions makers and big business; (3) nationalist ambitions and antagonisms, which "had contributed happily to the unification of Germany and Italy" but "had disrupted the Ottoman Empire and threatened to disrupt the Hapsburg Monarchy", (4) economic imperialism, which resulted in international rivalry for markets, raw materials, and colonies, but which is "usually exaggerated as one of the underlying causes of the War"; and (5) the newspaper press in all the great countries, a factor much greater than commonly supposed, which was "inclined to inflame nationalistic feelings, misrepresent the situation in foreign countries, and suppress factors in favor of peace."[48]

As necessary as such underlying causes may have been, however, Fay is not willing to abandon the notion of individual responsibility, in either the short run or the long. "After all," he writes, "the 'system' was worked by individuals; their personal acts built it up and caused it to explode in 1914. In the discussion of the future, it will be the work of the historians to explain the political, economic, and psychological motives which caused these individuals to act as they did."[49]

It is such statements as these that demonstrate Fay's ultimate reliance on social-psychological concepts. For, despite his ready references to alliance systems, arms races, nationalism, and pressure groups, the author consistently pictures the meaning of these factors in terms of the misperception and misunderstanding they caused in the minds of the European peoples and leaders. Thus, secret alliances "gradually divided Europe into two hostile groups of powers who were increasingly suspicious." And though armaments were alleged to be for defense, "what they really did was produce universal suspicion, fear, and hatred between nations." Nationalism also "nourished hatred," as did Fay's

48. Fay, *The Origins of the World War*, I, pp. 32-49.
49. *Ibid.*, I, p. 2.

particular *bête noire*, the newspaper press. It is Fay's opinion that "newspapers of two countries often took up some point of dispute, exaggerated it, and made attacks and counter-attacks, until a regular newspaper war was engendered, which thoroughly poisoned public opinion, and so offered a fertile soil in which the seeds of real war might easily germinate."[50]

As far as the leaders of Europe were concerned, Fay finds in them only the same myopia, suspicion, and tendency to panic that he detected in the nations at large. Even as sincere and reasonable a person as Sir Edward Grey (the British Foreign Minister) seems to him guilty of "deep-rooted suspicion" toward Germany. The author's judgment of French President Raymond Poincaré is still more severe: "He [Poincaré] believed a European War 'inevitable,'" Fay writes, and "in tightening the Entente and in making promises to Russia he did in fact tend to make it inevitable." Sergei Sazanov, the Russian Foreign Minister, Fay describes as "mercurial and emotional," a man who at the crucial moment "became thoroughly pessimistic, [and] jumped nervously to the conclusion that a European conflict was probably inevitable and that Russia should order mobilization." Wilhelm II possessed an "emotional and excitable mind," while Bethmann-Hollweg, the German Chancellor, was "idealistic and weak." It was the Kaiser's and Chancellor's rage at the Archduke's murder and their fear of Austrian dissolution that led them to their "leap in the dark"; but in reality they were "simpletons putting 'a noose about their necks,' and handing the other end of the rope to a stupid and clumsy adventurer" (Count Leopold Berchtold, Austrian Foreign Minister).[51]

Fay is not saying that all that Europe needed in order to avoid the terrible conflagration was a better set of "crisis managers." He sees the issues and problems as deeper than

50. *Ibid.*, I, pp. 34, 39, 44, 47, 48.
51. *Ibid.*, I, pp. 25, 31, 262, 264, II, pp. 206, 223, 440.

that. There is a glimmering of structural-functionalism in his recognition of the importance of alliance polarization in triggering an arms race and increased tension. There is also a touch of the group conflict perspective in his tendency to single out specific bodies like the military or communications media as guilty of exceeding the bounds of their appointed roles. Yet Fay never spells out in detail just how the absence of integration in the international system might have set up a growing competition between states; nor does he explain why certain groups within a society might have moved to violate that society's pluralism. He is content, after experimenting with several liberal perspectives, to bring the disparate events together primarily in terms of the misperception and distrust he believes they engendered. Thus for Fay the crisis of 1914 was finally the indispensable ingredient. As he put it on the last page of his book: "It is very doubtful whether all these dangerous tendencies would have actually led to war, had it not been for the assassination of Franz Ferdinand. That was the factor which consolidated the elements of hostility and started the rapid and complicated succession of events [on their way]."[52]

In turning to Ole Holsti, the second of our two authors, we encounter an even greater willingness than with Fay to focus on the immediate crisis itself. To be sure, in his book *Crisis Escalation War* (1972) Holsti explicitly disavows any intention of reopening "the issue of who was to blame for the catastrophe of 1914." He also makes very clear his belief that "not all crises result in war, nor do all wars arise from crises that get out of control."[53] Nevertheless, Holsti is obviously convinced that it is the interacting behavior in the last stages of a prewar period that makes all the difference as to whether the war ensues. In a paper which he authored jointly with Robert North and Richard Brody in 1964 while a member of North's Conflict and Integration Project at

52. *Ibid.*, II, p. 558.
53. Ole Holsti, *Crisis Escalation War* (Montreal: McGill-Queen's University Press, 1972), pp. 3, 237.

Stanford University, Holsti identified the typical chain of events leading to war as a rapid "conflict spiral" involving at least two parties and three features: burgeoning tensions, rising military preparedness, and increasingly hostile actions.[54] Later, in his book, Holsti spelled out what he had learned about the 1914 crisis in particular:

With increasing stress there was a vast increase in communication; information which did not conform to expectations and preferences was often disregarded or rejected; time pressure became an increasingly salient factor in policy making; attention became focused on the immediate rather than the longer-range consequences of actions; and one's alternatives and those of allies were viewed as limited and becoming more restricted . . . , whereas those of the adversary were believed to be relatively free from constraints.[55]

There is thus a tendency in Holsti's work, in part dictated by his primary interest in "policy making in high stress situations," to view all European statesmen of this era as victims of the same historical process. As he asserts at one point, "there are far greater and more consistent differences in perceptions of international hostility between one time period and the other [during July 1914] than there are between individuals in any nation."[56] Or, as he concludes forgivingly, "men rarely perform at their best under stress."[57] To be sure, this does not lead Hoslti to fatalism or despair; on the contrary, his analysis of later international crises (including some that did not result in war) brings him to suggest a number of procedural steps that might improve

54. Robert C. North, Richard A. Brody, and Ole Holsti, "Some Empirical Data on the Conflict Spiral," *Peace Research Society (International) Papers*, 1 (1964).

55. Holsti, *Crisis Escalation War*, p. 200.

56. *Ibid.*, p. 74. At another point Holsti writes: "Though imperial ambitions, trade rivalries, arms races, alliances, and rigid military plans . . . and many other attributes of the international system in 1914 were potent factors in shaping and constraining European diplomacy, . . . the outbreak of war was the result of decisions which were made—or not made—by statesmen . . . and the evidence indicates that general war in 1914 was not the goal of any [of the] European leaders." *Ibid.*, p. 25.

57. *Ibid.*, p. 199.

the chances of governments finding alternative policies to fighting.[58] Still, Holsti's approach to World War I, like other social-psychological interpretations, tends to blur the sociopolitical economic distinctions between the nations involved in the struggle. Because it is so much more centered on the crisis experience than Fay's volume, it gives the reader a better picture of what a crisis can do to participants. On the other hand, Fay's study does far more justice to the idiosyncratic images and stereotypes possessed by the various nations and rulers in 1914.

The Structural-Functional Interpretation: G. Lowes Dickinson. It may seem strange to select as an example of a structural-functional interpretation of World War I a study that was done even before the theory was formally articulated, but there is a logic to the choice. Like all social theory, structural-functional thought grew out of a tradition that had long been in development. It also grew out of a mood that seems to recur from time to time in the evolution of any way of thinking.

In the case of structural-functionalism, of course, the contextual tradition was that of liberalism while the relevant mood was that of optimism. Despite the onset of the Cold War and in part perhaps because of the Allied triumph in World War II, Talcott Parsons and other structural-functionalists were able during the 1940s and 1950s to envision a world in which things normally worked together, in which the parts of the whole were becoming steadily more integrated and mutually accommodating. Their confidence is faintly reminiscent of that of Adam Smith, that great eighteenth-century optimist who in first articulating liberal economic thought assumed that the self-interest of individuals would generally add up to the good of all men.

The era of World War I was another occasion on which liberal optimism came to the fore. In particular the American president Woodrow Wilson was representative of this,

58. *Ibid.*, pp. 204-237.

so much so that to this day the adjective "Wilsonian" is used to describe liberal foreign policy at its idealistic, interventionistic, and naive extreme. Driven by a profound belief in God's benevolence and America's mission, Wilson became supremely committed to the idea of using the war as a means to liberalize and tie together the belligerent nations, thus, in his words, making it "a war to end all wars," "a war to make the world safe for democracy."[59]

Wilson's plans for the future were, not surprisingly, closely linked to his interpretation of what had caused the war in the beginning. The emphasis that he placed upon self-determination of peoples, for example, as well as his demand for "open covenants, openly arrived at," can be traced to his conviction that nondemocratic groups and structures had contributed greatly to prewar dissatisfactions and hatreds. His insistence on "freedom of the seas" and the "free, constant, unthreatened intercourse of nations" was in response to his own experience with the perils of neutrality.[60]

Above all, however, it was with the foundation of a league of nations that Wilson hoped to draw the world into a new era of cooperation, mutuality, and equilibrium. "There must be, not a balance of power," he wrote, "but a community of power; not organized rivalries, but an organized common peace." One can see the events of 1914 flash before Wilson's eyes as he sums up the case for the league: "I am proposing that all nations henceforth avoid entangling alliances which would draw them into competitions of power; catch them in a net of intrigue and selfish rivalry, and disturb their own affairs with influences intruded from without. There is no entangling alliance in a concert of power."[61] For Wilson, then, the meaning of collective security lay in the creation of a system that was not divided against itself.

59. See Levin, *Woodrow Wilson and World Politics*, pp. 13-46.
60. Woodrow Wilson, speeches of January 22, 1917, and January 8, 1918, in E. David Cronon (ed.), *The Political Thought of Woodrow Wilson* (Indianapolis: Bobbs-Merrill, 1965), pp. 412, 438-445.
61. Wilson, speech of January 22, 1917, in Cronon, *The Political Thought of Woodrow Wilson*, pp. 410, 414.

Wilson's ideas and program could hardly have found a more ardent or eloquent champion during the postwar period than the British publicist, G. Lowes Dickinson (1862-1932). A graduate and fellow of King's College, Cambridge, Dickinson was widely known for his intelligent and critical commentary on philosophical, historical, and literary subjects. He was the author of over twenty books, including works on French history, Asian civilization, and modern religion. For more than a decade after 1914, however, his primary interest was in explaining the war and prescribing a way to avoid its repetition.[62]

The International Anarchy, 1900-1914, published in 1926, was the last and most ambitious of Dickinson's attempts to deal with the recent conflict. In this volume, born of the conviction that modern war "has become incompatible with the continuance of civilization," Dickinson offers the reader the thesis that, though mankind is not condemned to war, "whenever and wherever the anarchy of armed states exists, war does become inevitable." In such a situation, Dickinson contends, states will necessarily pursue a favorable balance of power, aiming to establish alliances that are "sufficiently stronger than [any] other to dictate rather than accept results." Maintaining the balance of power, then, is in reality a perpetual effort to get the better of the balance; and as this effort is prosecuted on both sides, the ultimate issue is war."[63]

The author explains in detail why this is so. Noting that balance of power politics leads directly to competition in military expenditures, he goes on to point out that "under such conditions there can be no real possibility of a permanent limitation of armaments." Moreover, the anarchy of

62. Among Dickinson's books on the subject were *The European Anarchy* (New York: Macmillan, 1916), *The Choice Before Us* (New York: Dodd, Mead, 1917), and *Causes of International War* (New York: Harcourt, Brace and Howe, 1920).

63. Dickinson, *The International Anarchy, 1904-1914* (New York: Century, 1926) pp. v, 5, 6.

international relations justifies a national expansionism which caters to the ignorance, indifference, ambition, and acquisitiveness of human beings. Finally, the armed anarchy defeats the good intentions of even the most admirable of men. Such a situation, "where forces are always ready to break loose and secrecy is therefore essential, is not compatible with honesty." Diplomats are therefore forced into fraudulent and destructive behavior.[64]

In turning to the specifically historical, Dickinson (as you would expect of a systems analyst) tends to put the emphasis on long-term factors. He begins his discussion with the rise of Germany to great power status after 1870, an event which ended by altering the relations of Britain to France and Russia. "For some time the signs pointed to an Anglo-German alliance," he notes, but "this proved impracticable, partly because, in the earlier phases, Britain was not (as the Germans neatly put it) *Bundnissreif* (alliable), partly because, in the later years, her intentions seemed to be to use Germany as a cat's-paw in a British war against Russia." As it turned out, England in a sudden shift, moved to ally with France, and France with England. This alteration, which triggered a similar rapprochement with Russia, transformed the balance of power into something "both singularly simple and singularly precarious." The history of the following years was to Dickinson "but that of [the] posturings of the combatants, their hesitations and fears, their taking and abandoning of positions, before they [were] ripe for the great decision."[65]

For Dickinson the lessons and the message of the war are obvious. Despite the rise of new leadership and other war-induced changes, the only "way to salvation is the development of the League of Nations into a true international organ to control in the interests of peace the foreign policies of all States." It was to persuade students of both the peril and the remedy, Dickinson says, that his book was written.[66]

64. *Ibid.*, pp. 10, 12-17, 37.   65. *Ibid.*, pp. 71-72.   66. *Ibid.*, p. 478.

Here, then, is an explanation of the coming of World War I with a moral but with no heroes or villains. Like other authors of structural-functional inclinations, Dickinson makes the human figures of his story seem almost dispensable. It is not that there were not fears, suspicions, and misperceptions at work. (Indeed, their presence might lead the reader to hypothesize that the social-psychological and structural-functional approaches are ultimately reconcilable.) Nor is it the case that Dickinson invariably ignores economic factors ("seizure of territory, a principal motive for war, has been prompted, among other things, by the desire to acquire important raw materials or potential or actual markets") or finds human nature praiseworthy ("the people go . . . like sheep to the slaughter").[67] Yet when the tale is told, for Dickinson the basic problem lies with the system, or rather, with the holding fast to an old system when the world is ready for a better one.

The Group Conflict Interpretation: Fritz Fischer and Gerhard Ritter. One would not expect to find Fritz Fischer (1908-   ) and his arch rival, Gerhard Ritter (1888-1967), in the same category of theory, much less a liberal category. After all, Fischer's attack on the dominant historiography of World War I during the 1960s was considered by many to be radical, even Marxist in its orientation, while Ritter's defense of Germany's innocence was described again and again as essentially conservative. Nevertheless, upon closer scrutiny, it becomes clear that the two historians have a number of critical group conflict assumptions in common.

In demonstrating how this is possible, we can most easily begin by examining the writings of Fischer, since in recent years it is around his thesis that the issues have usually been defined. Ritter was twenty years Fischer's senior and a well-established professor long before the Nazi period; even so, his scholarly statements on the coming of the war were approximately contemporaneous with Fischer's, and his

67. *Ibid.*, pp. 17, 22.

position becomes more understandable when we place it alongside that of the Hamburg historian.

A relatively unknown scholar when his first book touched Germany's "raw nerve" in 1961, Fritz Fischer spent the better part of the following decade defending himself against his critics and developing his interpretation.[68] *Germany's Aims in the First World War* dealt only in passing with the causes of the conflict (being focused on the years following 1914), but enough had been said about the subject to stimulate intense reactions. In *World Power or Decline* (1965) Fischer responded to factual and methodological criticism by attempting to lay out and refine the central assertions of his earlier work.[69] Finally, in *War of Illusions* (1969) he turned his full attention on the immediate prewar period, presenting and documenting his case in detail, and in a certain sense radicalizing it.

One of the more obvious and consistent things about Fischer's view of 1914 is a tone of anger and indignation at German behavior. Fischer clearly blames Germany for the war, and in particular he blames what he sees as a continuing, conscious, and aggressive German nationalism. It is this emphasis on continuity, of course, that offended many contemporary Germans who were eager to treat the nationalistic excesses of the Hitler years as an historical aberration. And it is Fischer's anger that led a number of observers to describe the professor's approach to the German past as basically ethical or moralistic.[70]

Yet despite a tendency on Fischer's part to utilize personalistic and psychological terms in seeming to accuse almost the entire German nation of an obsession with power, there

68. See Konrad H. Jarausch, "World Power or Tragic Fate? The Kriegschuldfrage as Historical Neurosis," *Central European History*, 5 (March 1972), pp. 72-92. See also Mommsen, "Domestic Factors in German Foreign Policy."

69. Fritz Fischer, *World Power or Decline* (New York: W. W. Norton, 1974; first published in German in 1965).

70. See, for example, Mommsen, "The Debate on German War Aims," p. 54.

is more than this to the author's position. Even in his earliest work Fischer pointed out that it was principally the army, heavy industry, and wide sections of the upper middle class which championed the most outrageous of the imperialist objectives.[71] In his second book, in 1965, he noted that "the expansionist war aims of Germany's political and economic forces were . . . designed to defend her traditional social structure against the threatening forces of democracy."[72] In *War of Illusions* Fischer is still more explicit: "In leading circles it was hoped that an aggressive foreign policy would reinforce the threatened social status quo and that Weltpolitik and national Machtpolitik could be used as a means of reducing social tensions at home by diverting attention to the outside world."[73] He supplements this statement with the observation that, during the economic difficulties of 1913-1914, "the close contacts which existed between the army and the politicians, between the industrial and commercial leadership and the government made the fear that Germany would not be allowed to expand universally accepted. The government was now under increasingly strong pressure from various interested groups [to do something]."[74] Thus Fischer offers us a group conflict theory (with radical overtones) in which organized groups (including capitalists) help to create and use a reckless foreign policy to protect and further their own interests.

Still, it would be an exaggeration to claim real consistency for Fischer's presentation. As one of his reviewers remarked, his "arguments constantly shift, charging at times one group, at times another with warlike tendencies. . . . And he does not claim that the various groups and persons with whom he is dealing were all, and at all times, committed to go to war."[75] Moreover, there is no precise connection established

71. Fischer, *Germany's Aims*, pp. 3-98.
72. Fischer, *World Power or Decline*, p. 82.
73. Fischer, *War of Illusions*, p. 258.
74. *Ibid.*, p. 443.
75. Mommsen, "Domestic Factors in German Foreign Policy," p. 12.

between pressures exerted and governmental decisions taken. Fischer does demonstrate the existence of substantial right wing mobilization on the eve of the war, for example, but he fails to show why this (or any other factor) would necessarily mean that "the war which the German politicians started in July 1914 was not a preventive war fought out of 'fear and despair' . . . [but rather an attempt] to realize Germany's political ambitions which may be summed up as German hegemony over Europe."[76] Fischer seems to want to have the best of several worlds, with capitalists driven by fear of losing markets (a radical view), a variety of reactionary and conservative groups attempting through foreign policy to preserve their positions (a group conflict view), the nation at large infected with nationalism and ambition (a social-psychological or possibly radical view if the capitalists are responsible for bamboozling the workers, about which Fischer is not clear), and finally, a political leadership unwilling to forego the chance to achieve European hegemony (perhaps a conservative view). All of this takes place in a world in which, according to Fischer, other industrial nations have more successfully "integrated" the workers' movement and the bourgeois states are therefore pursuing less aggressive foreign policies than Germany's.[77]

There was something to stir up almost everyone in Fischer's interpretation, and Gerhard Ritter, professor of history at Freiburg (1924-1956, except during his arrest by the Gestapo, 1944-45), was certainly among those who were upset. He was old enough to remember personally the mood and feelings of 1914, and his recollections were much more charitable than Fischer's reconstruction. This is not to say that he was uncritical of the historical actors involved. In fact, in the preface to Volume II of his *The Sword and the Scepter* (in which, several months before the publication of Fischer's 1961 book, he first discussed in detail the coming of the war) Ritter had remarked that "for most of my life

76. Fischer, *War of Illusions*, p. 470.
77. *Ibid.*, p. 258.

... [the prewar Germany of my youth] ... seemed to me to be bathed in a kind of radiance that did not begin to darken until the outbreak of war in 1914. Now, at the twilight of my life, my probing eye finds shadows far deeper than my generation perceived—let alone my academic teachers."[78]

What then was Ritter's point of view? He was often called a conservative, and there is a large element of truth in such a characterization.[79] Ritter was cautious of generalization, preferring to emphasize the complexity of history and the extent to which it is beyond human control. This is evidenced by his recurrent use, at critical moments in his writing, of concepts like fate, destiny, and tragedy.[80] It is also indicated by his implicit and explicit suspicions, frequently expressed, of modern mass democracy. As he wrote in 1955, the possibility of totalitarian tyranny "grows where the great, socially disorganized, intellectually uniform masses in the modern city awaken to political consciousness, and where the former public authorities with their roots in the dim past (monarchy or parliamentary government) are destroyed or discredited."[81] Small wonder that Ritter's books, from his early work on Luther and Stein to his postwar study of Carl Goerdler (a conservative leader in the resistance to Hitler), are sometimes described as celebrations of German tradition![82]

Yet there was another side to Ritter—one which came increasingly to the fore in the years after 1945 and which, as intimated above, led him into a more and more hostile stance with regard to the Wilhelminian period. This liberal side of the man, which appears in such remarks as his description of nineteenth-century British parliamentarian-

78. Ritter, *The Sword and the Scepter*, II, p. 2.

79. See Iggers, *New Directions in European Historiography*, pp. 89, 108, 114.

80. See, for example, *The Sword and the Scepter*, II, pp. 247, 75. See also Fischer, *World Power or Decline*, p. 124.

81. Gerhard Ritter, "The Historical Foundations of the Rise of National-Socialism," in Maurice Baumont *et al.* (eds.), *The Third Reich* (New York: Frederick A. Praeger, 1955), pp. 396-397.

82. See Joll, "The 1914 Debate Continues," pp. 22-28.

ism as a "just balancing of the opposing desires and interests of different classes, groups, and individuals,"[83] also makes itself evident in his choice of a subject for his magnum opus: the problem of militarism in Germany (which is the subtitle of *The Sword and the Scepter*). In the second volume of this series his liberalism brought him to a vigorous condemnation of the idiosyncratic constitutional structure of the German Empire, the excessive prestige enjoyed by the military among the leading strata of German society, and the folly of the naval building program. In Ritter's opinion, militarism, or the emancipation of the military power from the political leadership, was a comparatively recent (that is to say, post-Bismarckian) event in German history,[84] but such a view did not prevent him from seeing certain roots of the problem in the period before 1890.[85] What Ritter had developed was a group conflict analysis with a military component that had gotten out of control, lost its sense of subordination and proportion, and perverted the attitude of the natural countervailing groups.

Given such a picture of the situation, it is not surprising that Ritter was incensed at the interpretation of World War I that Fritz Fischer presented. Ritter was quick to admit that the older German literature on the subject had been "all too apologetic," but from his standpoint Fischer had gone to the other extreme in constructing "a new war guilt thesis."[86] He attacked Fischer bitterly on several counts, specifically for (1) seeing a German conspiracy to wage aggressive war when none had existed, (2) underestimating the extent to which

83. Baumont *et al.*, *The Third Reich*, p. 395.
84. Ritter, *The Sword and the Scepter*, II, pp. 93-98. See also Klaus Epstein, "Gerhard Ritter and the First World War," in H. W. Koch (ed.), *The Origins of the First World War* (London: Macmillan, 1972), pp. 289-294.
85. See, for example, *The Sword and the Scepter*, II, pp. 93-104, 119-136.
86. Gerhard Ritter, "A New War Guilt Thesis?" in Dwight E. Lee (ed.), *The Outbreak of the First World War: Causes and Responsibilities*, 4th ed. (Lexington, Mass.: D. C. Heath, 1975; essay originally published in German in June 1962), pp. 97-98.

Austria-Hungary was responsible for its own actions in the July crisis, (3) failing to realize that the German war aims enunciated after August 1914 reflected the impact of war more than prewar desires, (4) not carrying out significant research with regard to the actions of other nations, and (5) presenting his narrative in a generally biased and careless way. In particular Ritter objected to Fischer's treatment of Chancellor Bethmann-Hollweg, whom he had come to see not as an ambitious manipulator but as a person of decency and moderation caught in an unenviable and tragic predicament.[87]

The essence of Bethmann-Hollweg's problem, according to Ritter, lay in the combination of institutional weakness and personal insecurity which made it possible for the military point of view to be registered too powerfully. Unable to balance out the military's influence by appealing to groups outside the government, unsure of himself when confronted by the expertise of generals and admirals, the Chancellor sank little by little during these years into a mood of gloomy fatalism about international relations.[88] The nightmare that confronted him (the "experts" said) was that while Austria-Hungary, Germany's last reliable ally, was growing steadily weaker and less mobile, Russia's military might was increasing apace. His conclusion in July 1914 was that he must risk "a leap in the dark" in order to preclude the possibility of a decades-long decline in Germany's status as a great power. "In sum," argued Ritter, "the Chancellor's decisions to side with Austria-Hungary even at the risk of a European war can be called an act of desperate resolve rather than of arrogant faith in victory."[89] In this way the historian builds his interpretation largely on the

87. *Ibid.*, pp. 102-107.
88. See the Supplement to the Notes to Chapter 10 in *The Sword and the Scepter*, II, pp. 315-318. See also Gerhard Ritter, *The German Problem: Basic Questions of German Political Life, Past and Present* (Columbus: Ohio State University Press, 1965; a translation of the second German edition, published 1962), pp. 151-194.
89. Ritter, *The Sword and the Scepter*, II, p. 316.

basis of group conflict theory (both at the domestic and international levels), almost unconsciously tempering it with social-psychological (misperception) perspectives and a conservative sense of pathos. It is the mood of Ritter's writing, certainly more than the theory involved, that differentiates it from that of Fischer.

The Radical Tradition and World War I Historiography: Fritz Klein and Konni Zilliacus

In taking up the radical history of our subject we have chosen to examine the work of a German Marxist-Leninist under the rubric of the orthodox "class conflict" perspective and of a left wing British Labourite within the category of "revisionist" scholarship. Since Marxist-Leninist (or Communist) theory is older, simpler, and more precisely defined than relevant Social Democratic theory, we have selected that category as the point of reference from which to depart. Ironically, however, because the Marxist-Leninist tradition has taken a longer time to produce what from the Western point of view would be called "sophisticated" history, the Communist chosen is of a later generation than the Social Democrat with whom he is paired.[90]

The Orthodox Class Conflict Interpretation: Fritz Klein. In a real sense, of course, Lenin himself was the first Marxist-Leninist historian of World War I.[91] Just as Karl Marx had worked out a theory of revolution in response to the revolutions of 1848 (with the result that to this day there seems to be a remarkably good "fit" between Marxist theory and the history of that event), so Lenin developed his own ideas about imperialism and war while experiencing and observing the international competitions of the early twen-

90. On the development of Communist historical writing, see Iggers, *New Directions in European Historiography*, pp. 123-152.

91. See, in particular, V. I. Lenin, *Imperialism, the Highest Stage of Capitalism* (New York: International Publishers, 1939; first published in 1916). See also *Lenin on War and Peace: Three Articles* (Peking: Foreign Language Press, 1966; first published 1915-1924).

124 HISTORIANS AND WORLD WAR I

tieth century. The consequences for future Marxist history and historians were understandably double-edged. It was obviously advantageous to have the insight and interpretation of the period from the master craftsman of the world Communist movement. On the other hand, it was also considerably inhibiting, even if one were free to express oneself (which was not always the case), to be faced with the challenge of trying to improve upon the analysis of the master. The temptation to parrot Lenin's statements and formulas was a severe one, and was not frequently resisted. It was only with the decade of the 1960s, under the impact of the controversy generated by Fritz Fischer in West Germany, that Communist scholars were inspired to supplement and clarify (but not yet criticize) Lenin's historical analysis of World War I.

Professor Fritz Klein (1924-   ) of the Central Institute for History of the Academy of Sciences in East Berlin has been a leader in this effort. An editor and productive scholar for more than 25 years, Klein published his first book in 1952 on interwar relations between the Soviet Union and Germany,[92] and followed this up in 1961-62 with two volumes on German history from the 1890s through the Armistice of 1918.[93] In 1964, the year that the Fischer controversy reached its peak, he turned his attention specifically to the causes of the First World War,[94] and in succeeding years, while directing a team of scholars working on a massive study of the entire war period, he continued to research that topic. His findings have been published as chapters in Volume I of the resulting *Deutschland im ersten Weltkrieg* (three volumes, 1968-1970) and subsequently, in shorter form, as part of the account by Klein, Willibald Gutsche,

92. Fritz Klein, *Die Diplomatische Beziehungen Deutschlands zur Sovietunion 1917-1932* (Berlin: Rütten & Loenig, 1952).

93. Fritz Klein, *Deutschland von 1897/98 bis 1917* (Berlin: Deutscher Verlag der Wissenschaften, 1966); and Klein, *Deutschland 1918* (Berlin: Rütten & Loenig, 1961).

94. Fritz Klein, *Es begann in Sarajevo* (Berlin: Akademie Verlag, 1964).

and Joachim Petzold entitled *Von Sarajevo nach Versailles.*[95]

As one would expect with an influential scholar from a Communist country, the framework of Klein's analysis conforms in general to that laid down by Lenin. The basic problem of the period, as he describes it, is that the nations of Europe, having entered "the stage of finance capitalism," were inevitably being drawn into competitive imperialist activities that could only end in international conflict. In Klein's own words: "The newly maturing capitalism of the developed lands, organized in mighty monopolies, striving incessantly for higher profits and therefore for steady expansion, carried on a wild and reckless struggle over new markets [and] over economic and political advantages." The result was a complicated series of interrelated colonial wars, interstate clashes, and class violence—"a whole bundle of steadily worsening contradictions and tensions" out of which the Great War arose.[96] Or as Klein puts it at another point, "The First World War was an imperialist war on the part of all participating nations."[97]

Even so, it is an interesting fact that, following up on the Leninist insight that "the development of capitalism occurs unevenly in the various countries," Klein proceeds to draw greater distinctions regarding the responsibility for the war among the belligerents than Lenin himself did at the time.[98] In Klein's view it is clear that "German imperialism [bears] a

95. Willibald Gutsche, Fritz Klein, and Joachim Petzold, *Von Sarajevo nach Versailles: Deutschland im ersten Weltkrieg* (Berlin: Akademie Verlag, 1974). This book is based not only upon Volume I of *Deutschland im ersten Weltkrieg* (fully cited in footnote 22, above), but also upon Volume II (*Januar 1915 bis Oktober 1917*), published in 1969, and Volume III (*November 1917 bis November 1918*), published in 1970.

96. Gutsche, Klein, and Petzold, *Von Sarajevo nach Versailles*, pp. 11-12.

97. *Ibid.*, p. 51.

98. *Ibid.*, p. 12. Note that Lenin, in emphasizing the uneven development of capitalist states, was attempting to explain why a proletarian revolution might occur in certain nations before others; he did not use this insight to justify blaming one capitalist state more than the others for the war. See *Lenin on War and Peace*, pp. 6-12, 22.

special responsibility for bringing about and triggering [the war]."[99] German foreign policy was particularly aggressive, he believes, because Germany, handicapped by late unification and industrialization, had not been able to obtain a share of the imperialist spoils commensurate with its rapidly increasing economic power. Russia, France, and Britain were admittedly far from innocent (Russia was more and more antagonistic to growing German influence in Turkey while at the same time increasingly desirous of gaining control of the Straits), but they were to a great degree in the position of defending what they already possessed.[100]

None of this should imply that Klein is able to write only about abstractions like capitalists, classes, or nation-states. On the contrary, his rendition of events reveals a surprising (almost bourgeois) amount of attention to individuals and groups within the larger groups. William II, Bethmann-Hollweg, Berchtold, and other European leaders play prominent roles in the story.[101] So does the military leadership of the Central Powers, which according to Klein was the "earliest and most emphatic influence in pressing [those countries] into war."[102] Occasionally Klein even points up disagreements and visions within allegedly dominant classes, as when he notes that during the crucial summer weeks Lord Grey was forced to pursue a cautious foreign policy because "influential circles of the English bourgeoisie were against [Britain's] getting into the conflict."[103]

A noteworthy, if not completely unexpected, aspect of Klein's work is the interest he displays in the German anti-war movement during the July crisis, particularly as reflected in the activities of the workers' organizations and socialist party.[104] Here Klein is intent on demonstrating that the workers, though genuinely aroused to protest what was

99. Klein, *Deutschland im ersten Weltkrieg*, I, p. 295. See also Gutsche, Klein, and Petzold, *Von Sarajevo nach Versailles*, pp. 13, 51.
100. Klein, *Deutschland im ersten Weltkrieg*, I, pp. 241-248.
101. See *ibid.*, pp. 212-240.
102. *Ibid.*, p. 215.   103. *Ibid.*, p. 245.   104. *Ibid.*, pp. 259-277.

occurring, were relatively helpless in the face of a repressive and well-organized government as well as the tendency of their own "reformist" and "opportunist" party leaders to compromise. The outlawing of street demonstrations was extremely inhibiting, Klein contends, "but the fatal blow to the anti-war movement of the proletariat in July 1914 was [the cooperation rendered the establishment] by the right-wing Social Democratic leaders themselves."[105] Having said this, however, Klein is at pains to show how adroit it was of Bethmann-Hollweg to have the war credits bill brought to discussion and vote in the Reichstag during August 1-3, when Germany was already at war with reactionary Russia but not yet fighting with France or England.[106]

All in all, even giving Klein his assumptions and admitting his impressive research, his overall argument is not as powerful as it might be. Primarily this is because the author never makes a case for the various governments really being at the mercy of the capitalists. True, he does point out the rather startling fact that the Kaiser had dinner with Friedrich Alfred Krupp, "the most important man in the German armaments industry," on the evening of July 6, the day after he had informed the Austrians of his unqualified support.[107] Moreover, Klein identifies quite specifically a number of German banks and firms that he claims were significant in pushing the Berlin government into expansionist moves.[108] Nevertheless, he does not systematically isolate and test Marxist-Leninist hypotheses about the situation, as one would assume he would do if he were sufficiently aware that he is dealing with what is only a theory. Klein does not even make an attempt to establish the sort of data that the British economic historian J. A. Hobson was able to provide in his book *Imperialism: A Study* as early as 1902. Indeed, the

105. *Ibid.*, p. 268.
106. Gutsche, Klein, and Petzold, *Von Sarajevo nach Versailles*, pp. 45-48.
107. Klein, *Deutschland im ersten Weltkrieg*, I, pp. 222.
108. Gutsche, Klein, and Petzold, *Von Sarajevo nach Versailles*, pp. 13-14.

paramount difficulty with Klein's work is not, as one reviewer asserts, that "the Marxist-Leninist pattern is too general" for historians to use,[109] but rather that Klein has not faced up to the kinds of questions his theory required him to ask and the kinds of proof necessary for persuasive answers.

Having criticized Klein for remaining too much an old-fashioned diplomatic historian, it may be unfair to add that, even so, the personalities of his history often seem somewhat less than human. To be sure, he does picture Wilhelm II as "frivolous," Bethmann-Hollweg as "skeptical," and the socialist Haase as "demagogic," while the policies of German imperialists are diagnosed as "adventurous and illusionary."[110] Still, there is something remarkably bloodless and predictable about the behavior of the leading individuals. This may be nothing more than the self-conscious rationality that we naturally expect to find in the actors of radical interpretations. On the other hand, it may derive from the author's minimizing more than necessary the varieties possible even within a small range of interest or conditioning.

The Revisionist Class Conflict Interpretation: Konni Zilliacus. The view that Konni Zilliacus offers us of World War I is similar to that of Fritz Klein, yet subtly and significantly different. In one sense it is a more consistent picture, since Zilliacus tends to place the blame for the conflict more equally on all participating nations. In another sense the image created is less precise, since the author compounds the accusations he makes against capitalism with charges regarding international anarchy and power politics. The resulting composite is an interesting and accurate reflection of his complex personality and experience.

Zilliacus' life (1892-1967) was truly rich enough for three

109. Mommsen, "Domestic Factors in German Foreign Policy," p. 7.
110. Gutsche, Klein, and Petzold, *Von Sarajevo nach Versailles*, pp. 11, 49; Klein, *Deutschland im ersten Weltkrieg*, I, p. 223.

men. He was born in Kobe, Japan, to a Scottish-American
mother and a Swedish-Finnish father (also Konni Zilliacus),
a radical journalist who later smuggled arms to Finnish
nationalists and Russian revolutionaries during the Russo-
Japanese War. Young Zilliacus went to school in America,
Finland, Sweden, and England, but returned to the United
States to be graduated in 1915 from Yale at the top of his
class. Then, after serving for two years in the British Flying
Corps and subsequently in the British expeditionary force to
eastern Siberia, he took a position in the Information
Section of the League of Nations, where his mastery of eight
languages proved invaluable and where he specialized in
eastern European and Soviet affairs. During this period
(1919-1938) he also wrote prolifically, publishing pamphlets
and short books under the pseudonyms of Vigilantes, Diplomaticus, and Roth Williams.[111] In 1945 he was elected to
Parliament in the Labour Party landslide, but his term there
was not an easy one, for he found himself repeatedly
attacking Anglo-American foreign policy and in 1949 was
expelled from his party for voting against British entrance
into NATO. Defeated for reelection in 1950, he was re-
admitted to the Labour Party in 1952 and served again in
Parliament from 1955 to the time of his death. Called a
"crypto Communist" by conservatives, considered anathema
by the Soviet Union from 1948 to 1956 because of his open
admiration for Tito (about whom he wrote a biography),[112]
Zilliacus saw himself as a loyal and conscientious Social
Democrat. His political creed, expressed in 1949, was "that
Labour has come to fulfil the promise of Liberalism and

111. Among the publications by Vigilantes are *The Dying Peace* (Lon-
don: The New Statesman and Nation, 1933), *Abyssinia* (London: The New
Statesman and Nation, 1935), *Inquest on Peace* (London: V. Gollancz,
1935), and *Why We Are Losing the Peace* (London: V. Gollancz, 1939).
The writings by Diplomaticus include *The Czechs and Their Minorities*
(London: T. Butterworth, 1938) and *Can the Tories Win the Peace?*
(London: V. Gollancz, 1945). *The League of Nations Today* (London: G.
Allen and Unwin, 1923) and other works are attributed to Roth Williams.
112. Konni Zilliacus, *Tito of Yugoslavia* (London: Michael Joseph,
1952).

that, in advancing toward Socialism, increasing social justice and diminishing economic inequality and insecurity, we are laying the foundations of peace, enlarging the frontiers of liberty and approaching the good society."[113]

Zilliacus' analysis of the causes of World War I is found primarily in one book, *Mirror of the Past*, which he published at the end of World War II in an attempt to draw lessons from the earlier period which would help in avoiding a repetition of "mistakes" made at that time. Actually, *Mirror of the Past* and its sister volume *Mirror of the Present* (1947) were "both derived from the fourth revision of the big book I wrote and rewrote during my last ten years [with] the League of Nations Secretariat."[114] The first volume deals with the period 1900-1929; the second with the years 1929-1945.

There is obviously a strong element of liberal structural-functionalism in Zilliacus' perspective, revealed not only in his years of dedication to the League but also in his considerable emphasis on the dangers of the modern state system. Quoting G. Lowes Dickinson at some length, Zilliacus contends that existing "international anarchy is a vicious system that makes vicious conduct necessary and ultimately makes war inevitable, however good may be the intentions of the statesmen [involved]."[115] Though there has been a growing tendency toward interdependence of peoples, he says, it was not strong enough in the years before 1914 to offset the antagonisms inherent in the changing balance of power, shifting alliances, and burgeoning arms race.

But that is not all. It is not just a lack of international

113. Konni Zilliacus, *I Choose Peace* (Middlesex: Penguin Books, 1949), p. 14. The biographical background is from Konni Zilliacus, *Mirror of the Past: A History of Secret Diplomacy* (New York: Current Books, 1946; originally published as *The Mirror of the Past* in London in 1944), pp. xi-xx; Konni Zilliacus, *A New Birth of Freedom? World Communism after Stalin* (New York: Monthly Review Press, 1958), pp. 7-12; and Konni Zilliacus' obituary in the *New York Times*, July 7, 1967, p. 33.
114. Zilliacus, *Mirror of the Past*, p. xviii.
115. *Ibid.*, pp. 3-8.

integration that leads to war, according to Zilliacus, but also the fact that behind the facade of national power and organization in capitalist states there lurks a plutocracy of "very rich bankers and businessmen who [have] fused . . . with the remains of the landholding aristocracy."[116] In the late nineteenth century these bankers and businessmen, drawn by a need for new markets and fields for investments, had been "the driving force behind the new imperialism [of the Western powers]."[117] In Zilliacus' view, "the vested interest of the plutocracy, issuing in economic nationalism and imperialism, increasingly supplied the content of the conflicts of power politics out of which wars and war preparations arose."[118]

In the end, asserts Zilliacus (basing his conclusions on relatively little evidence), each of the European nations decided to wage a "preventive" war:

Each side was defending its imperialist interests by preventing the balance of power from being tipped in favor of its opponents. These imperialist interests were in the last analysis the private interests of finance and monopoly capital, which, through the influence of the plutocracy on governments and public opinion, were identified in the minds of the rulers with "national honor and vital interests." There were, of course, other factors in the situation, and the psychological process by which promoting vested interests . . . is transmuted in men's minds into loyalty to religious, philanthropic, and patriotic ideals is complex and largely unconscious.[119]

Not even the plutocrats were actually "guilty," however, according to Zilliacus:

These people did not believe in the rightness of what they were doing as much as they were unconscious of the possibility of doing differently. . . . Therefore the social dynamic of the drift to war operated below the threshold of their consciousness. . . . It followed that their attitude to war was fatalistic.[120]

As for the specific factors involved in the outbreak of war in 1914, the author comes to a surprising conclusion. The

116. *Ibid.*, p. 16.   117. *Ibid.*, p. 18.   118. *Ibid.*, p. 29.
119. *Ibid.*, p. 137.   120. *Ibid.*, p. 138.

only nation, the only leadership with any real freedom of action, in his opinion, turns out to have been the British! As much as Zilliacus appreciates the terrible dilemma that Lord Grey and the Liberals faced in trying to foster conciliation at the last moment, he is still intensely critical of their inability to make a clear and timely commitment to France. His conclusion is "that the shilly-shallying of the Liberal government during those fatal three weeks bears a crushing responsibility for the vast calamity."[121] Thus, while the German Communist Klein puts the primary blame on Germany for the war, the British Socialist Zilliacus sees Britain as the greatest culprit.

In sum, it would almost seem that Zilliacus presents the reader with a classic example of Marxist-Leninist analysis. The historical actors in his account, with rare exceptions, behave as puppets on the end of economic strings. The people at large suffer from having been given what a more theoretical Marxist would probably call a "false consciousness" of their own interests. The author is clearly in some respects not very far along the road that revisionist socialists have traveled during the twentieth century in rendering their perspective more flexible, less classbound, and less determinist. Indeed, at one point Zilliacus even makes light of the optimism with which Karl Kautsky had predicted that capitalists would be wise enough to learn to avoid war by cooperating across national boundaries![122] Nonetheless, at the last scrutiny, what enables us to view Zilliacus as more of a Social Democrat than not is his belief in the power of intelligence to ensure future peace by reaching and radicalizing public opinion. The minds of the masses may have been poisoned by the plutocrats in 1914, but he does not assume that they have to remain so.

121. *Ibid.*, p. 119.   122. *Ibid.*, p. 147.

CHAPTER FIVE

Historians and World War II

As we move from the interpretations of the origins of World War I to those of World War II, the parameters of analysis narrow to some extent. Granted, World War II historiography is vitally alive with controversy and intense debate. In the main, however, these occur well within a liberal framework. In the case of World War II the plans and actions of one charismatic leader, Adolf Hitler (and, on the American side, of Franklin D. Roosevelt), have served as a kind of magnet, drawing all but a few historical interpretations toward a narrow range of the ideological spectrum. Even the kind of left-liberal, socioeconomic analysis initiated by Fritz Fischer and others regarding the origins of World War I, while present "in the wings" in the writings of Charles Beard, has not yet moved to "center stage" in World War II historiography. Consequently, though conservative, semi-radical, and radical accounts do exist, liberal interpretations of the war's origins vastly predominate.

Historians of World War II are commonly categorized either as "orthodox" (sometimes called "interventionist") or "revisionist" (also labeled "isolationist"). These terms, while perhaps useful in explaining certain tendencies within World War II historiography, nevertheless tend to obscure important characteristics. For one thing, they may suggest a much broader ideological and theoretical range than really exists. For another, such categories do not encourage us to probe beneath the historical analyses for deeper, and often more significant, assumptions about human beings and society. Our task in this chapter, therefore, as in Chapter 4, is briefly to describe the existing framework of the war's historiography and then to present and illustrate our own. Our aim is to demonstrate the usefulness of an organization based on ideological and theoretical categories.

What has been called the "orthodox" view of events in the 1930s—as represented, for example, by Sir Lewis Namier's *Diplomatic Prelude, 1938-1939* (1948) and his *Europe in Decay, 1936-1940* (1950), as well as Sir Alan Bullock's *Hitler: A Study in Tyranny* (1952) and Walther Hofer's *War Premeditated, 1939* (1955)—has two major theses.[1] The first of these is that Hitler's continuing long-range goal, clearly articulated in *Mein Kampf* (1925), was to establish German hegemony in Europe. Had European statesmen paid sufficient attention to this early "blueprint for aggression," and had they been properly alert to Hitler's true intentions, the Führer's aggressive campaign for dominance could have been averted. Instead, Hitler was permitted to take Germany out of the League of Nations, embark on rearmament, reoccupy the Rhineland, and achieve the support of Italy and Japan. Subsequently, in the lamentable absence of British and French opposition, Germany proceeded to swallow Austria, the Sudetenland, Bohemia, and Moravia. For so-called orthodox or traditional historians, then, World War II was obviously caused by Hitler's premeditated, even maniacal, drive for European conquest, and perhaps world

1. Sir Lewis Namier, *Diplomatic Prelude, 1938-1939* (London: Macmillan, 1948); Namier, *Europe in Decay, 1936-1940* (London: Macmillan, 1950); Sir Alan Bullock, *Hitler: A Study in Tyranny*, rev. ed. (New York: Harper and Row, 1962); and Walther Hofer, *War Premeditated, 1939* (London: Thames and Hudson, 1955). See also G. A. Craig and Felix Gilbert (eds.), *The Diplomats, 1919-1939* (Princeton: Princeton University Press, 1953); Elizabeth Wiskemann, *The Rome-Berlin Axis: A Study in the Relations Between Hitler and Mussolini*, rev. ed. (London: Collins, 1962); and Esmonde M. Robertson, *Hitler's Pre-War Policy and Military Plans, 1933-1939* (London: Citadel Press, 1963).

conquest as well. This madman should have, indeed *could* have, been vigorously resisted even earlier than he finally was.

The reasons this did not occur are suggested by the second thesis of the orthodox interpretation—good examples of which may be found in J. W. Wheeler-Bennett's *Munich, Prologue to Tragedy* (1948) and A. L. Rowse's *Appeasement: A Study in Political Decline, 1933-1939* (1961)— according to which British and French leaders mistakenly assumed that to have peace they must first eliminate whatever "grievances" were provoking Hitler to behave aggressively.[2] This "odious policy of concessions" began in 1935 and 1936, when Germany's rearmament and its reoccupation of the Rhineland were excused as understandable responses to the devastating losses of World War I. In May 1937, after Neville Chamberlain became Prime Minister, the policy of appeasement was intensified. Lord Halifax at Berchtesgaden went so far as to express sympathy to Hitler for his nation's grievances and to praise Nazi Germany as "the bulwark of Europe against Bolshevism." On the basis of that meeting, according to the orthodox view, Hitler concluded that Britain would not attempt to preserve the existing settlement in central Europe and decided to step up German nationalist agitation in Danzig, Czechoslovakia, and Austria. When the "suffering" of the Germans in the Sudetenland later became intolerable to the Führer, the result was the notorious Munich Conference and the Allied-

2. J. W. Wheeler-Bennett, *Munich, Prologue to Tragedy* (London: Macmillan, 1948); and A. L. Rowse, *Appeasement: A Study in Political Decline, 1933-1939* (New York: W. W. Norton, 1961). Other accounts that are highly critical of Allied policy are William L. Shirer, *The Rise and Fall of the Third Reich* (New York: Simon and Schuster, 1960); Martin Gilbert and Richard Gott, *The Appeasers* (London: Weidenfeld and Nicholson, 1963); and Margaret George, *The Warped Vision: British Foreign Policy, 1933-1938* (Pittsburgh: University of Pittsburgh Press, 1965). Also see Robert Skidelsky, "Going to War with Germany: Between Revisionism and Orthodoxy," *Encounter*, 39 (July 1959), pp. 56-65; and D. C. Watt, "Appeasement, The Rise of a Revisionist School?" *The Political Quarterly*, 36 (April-June 1965), pp. 191-213.

German agreement on Czech partition, interpreted by Chamberlain and other leaders as Hitler's pledge of peace. Only with the invasion of Prague did the British and French appeasers finally realize the extent of their own deception by Hitler.

The "orthodox" interpretation was first seriously challenged with the publication in 1961 of A. J. P. Taylor's *The Origins of the Second World War*.[3] This highly controversial work (which will be discussed at greater length in this chapter) adopted a substantially different perspective on Hitler's foreign policy. Glorying in "revisionism," Taylor argued that the war resulted not from Hitler's megalomania but rather from his faulty political calculations and those of the Western allies. Far from a maniacal aberration, Hitler was presented as just another German leader simply continuing the expansionist policies of such predecessors as Bethmann-Hollweg and Stresemann. Taylor, in short, refused to shift the guilt from the Germans as a nation, or from Europeans in general, to Hitler as a leader.

Not surprisingly, especially in light of his earlier, more orthodox scholarship, Taylor outraged many people with his conclusions. *The Origins of the Second World War* prompted a series of scathing reviews, including an especially heated critique by Hugh Trevor-Roper, then Regius Professor of History at Oxford University.[4] To attack the existing interpretation of the origins of World War II, it would seem, was to attack the very accomplishments of that war. Particularly in Britain, where the war constituted a last heroic moment before the British Empire was superseded by

3. A. J. P. Taylor, *The Origins of the Second World War* (New York: Atheneum, 1961). See also the conservative revisionist accounts of William N. Medlicott in *Contemporary England, 1914-1964* (New York: D. McKay, 1967); and Medlicott, *British Foreign Policy Since Versailles, 1919-1963* (London: Methuen, 1968).

4. H. R. Trevor-Roper, "A. J. P. Taylor, Hitler and the War," *Encounter*, 17 (July 1961), pp. 88-96. Also see C. Robert Cole, "Critics of the Taylor View of History," in Esmonde M. Robertson (ed.), *The Origins of the Second World War* (London: Macmillan, 1971), pp. 142-157.

an American one, an argument such as Taylor's was fiercely resisted.

Interestingly, a similar struggle between the "orthodox" historians and "revisionists" had long been waged in the United States. Among American historians, of course, there had been more interest in the antecedents of Pearl Harbor in 1941 than in the causes of the European war in 1939. These trans-Atlantic studies, therefore, focus on the issue of American intervention and on the role of Franklin D. Roosevelt in the war against Japan.

As applied to the United States, the orthodox interpretation was expressed even during the course of the war in books such as Forrest Davis and Ernest K. Lindley's *How War Came* (1942), and was fully developed by the mid-1950s in Herbert Feis's *The Road to Pearl Harbor* (1950) and in two important works by William L. Langer and S. Everett Gleason, *The Challenge to Isolation, 1937-1940* (1952) and *The Undeclared War, 1940-1941* (1953).[5] Virtually ignoring internal, socioeconomic factors, these observers stressed instead the importance of politics and of external pressures on the United States. They described the period 1920-1940 as an American retreat into isolationism, a retreat reversed only because the threat of Nazi aggression forced a reluctant United States to fight for the survival of democracy and humane values. Roosevelt is portrayed as an internationalist who successfully resisted the efforts of isolationists struggling vainly to keep America from fulfilling its obligation to resist totalitarianism and restore peace to the world. From this perspective, Germany, Japan, and Italy are seen as evil

5. Forrest Davis and Ernest K. Lindley, *How War Came* (New York: Simon and Schuster, 1942); Herbert Feis, *The Road to Pearl Harbor* (Princeton: Princeton University Press, 1950); William L. Langer and S. Everett Gleason, *The Challenge to Isolation, 1937-1940* (New York: Harper and Bros., 1952); and Langer and Gleason, *The Undeclared War, 1940-1941* (New York: Harper and Bros., 1953). Other orthodox treatments include Robert E. Sherwood, *Roosevelt and Hopkins: An Intimate History* (New York, 1948); and Basil Rauch, *Roosevelt: From Munich to Pearl Harbor* (New York: Creative Age Press, 1950).

aggressors attempting to destroy the status quo, while the United States emerges as an innocent, peaceful bystander.[6] In the Cold War period, similarly, the Soviet Union and China are viewed by orthodox historians to be the equivalents of Nazi Germany, while the historical lessons of the 1930s are adopted to solve the problems of the postwar era. As an example of this tendency, not only among orthodox historians of World War II but political leaders as well, Secretary of State Dean Rusk fervently inquired in 1965 when explaining United States involvement in Vietnam: "Can those of us in this room forget the lesson that we had in this issue of war and peace when it was only 10 years from the seizure of Manchuria to Pearl Harbor; about 2 years from the seizure of Czechoslovakia to the outbreak of World War II in Western Europe?"[7]

Reflecting perhaps a latent American isolationism, revisionist rebuttals had been quickly forthcoming from both the Right and the Left. During the 1950s, Right revisionists such as Frederick Sanborn, Charles Tansill, and Robert Theobald alleged that the United States had been drawn into war by the devious British aided by Roosevelt's left wing advisors.[8] Left revisionists, such as Charles Beard in the late 1940s and Lloyd Gardner, Noam Chomsky, and Bruce

6. For analyses of this American version of the orthodox interpretation, see Wayne Cole, "American Entry into World War II: A Historiographical Appraisal," *Mississippi Valley Historical Review*, 43 (March 1957), pp. 595-617; Robert A. Divine, "Diplomatic Historians and World War II," in Divine (ed.), *Causes and Consequences of World War II* (Chicago: Quandrangle, 1969), pp. 3-30; and Robert Freeman Smith, "American Foreign Relations, 1920-1942," in Barton J. Bernstein (ed.), *Towards a New Past: Dissenting Essays in American History* (New York: Vintage, 1969), pp. 232-262.

7. Quoted by Robert Freeman Smith in "American Foreign Relations, 1920-1942," p. 255.

8. Frederick C. Sanborn, *Design for War: A Study of Secret Power Politics* (New York: Devin-Adair, 1951); Charles C. Tansill, *Back Door to War: The Roosevelt Foreign Policy, 1933-1941* (Chicago: Regnery, 1952); and Robert A. Theobald, *The Final Secret of Pearl Harbor: The Washington Contribution to the Japanese Attack* (New York: Devin-Adair, 1954). See also Harry Elmer Barnes, *Perpetual War for Perpetual Peace* (Caldwell, Idaho: Caxton, 1953).

Russett in the 1960s, questioned both the wisdom of United States involvement in that particular war and the aggressiveness of American foreign policy in general.[9] The two "schools" shared only a common goal of keeping the United States free from such foreign entanglements.

Recent scholarship on both issues—the origins of the European war in 1939 and the reasons for United States entry into the war in 1941—while predominantly orthodox, has been heavily influenced by revisionist arguments. While it is not our intention here to provide a complete survey of the available literature, we would list as important additions on the European side the following books: Christopher Thorne, *The Approach of War, 1938-1939* (1967), which analyzes the limits of what Britain and France could do; Raymond J. Sontag, *A Broken World, 1919-1939* (1971), which emphasizes the impact of World War I on the situation; William Carr, *Arms, Autarky and Aggression* (1972), which stresses the primacy in Germany of internal policy over foreign policy; Norman Rich, *Hitler's War Aims* (1973), which suggests that Hitler was driven to war against nations that played no part in his original ideological program; and Klaus Hildebrand, *The Foreign Policy of the Third Reich* (1973), which views Hitler's foreign policy as a logical extension of the aims of the German nation-state of 1871 (and which is discussed more fully at the conclusion of this chapter). With regard to the Pacific conflict we would take note of Robert J. C. Butow, *Tojo and the Coming of the War* (1961), a somewhat hostile study of Japanese policy; Dorothy Borg, *The United States and the Far Eastern Crisis of 1933-1938* (1964), an account emphasizing

9. Charles A. Beard, *American Foreign Policy in the Making, 1932-1940* (New Haven: Yale University Press, 1946); Beard, *President Roosevelt and the Coming of the War, 1941* (New Haven: Yale University Press, 1948); Lloyd Gardner, *Economic Aspects of New Deal Diplomacy* (Madison: University of Wisconsin Press, 1964); Noam Chomsky, *American Power and the New Mandarins* (New York: Pantheon, 1969); and Bruce M. Russett, *No Clear and Present Danger: A Skeptical View of U.S. Entry into World War II* (New York: Harper and Row, 1972).

American caution and moderation; Dorothy Borg and Shumpei Okamoto (eds.), *Pearl Harbor as History* (1973), a collection of essays which lay much blame on governmental bureaucracies; and Stephen E. Pelz, *Race to Pearl Harbor* (1974), an impressive analysis of a runaway naval race.[10]

A NEW INTERPRETIVE FRAMEWORK

As in Chapter 4, in attempting to move beyond the standard "orthodox" and "revisionist" categories for World War II historiography, we must be concerned not primarily with the *conclusions* certain historians have reached about the causes of that war (e.g., were Hitler and the Nazis responsible or were other factors paramount?), but rather with *the way they reached those conclusions*. In other words, we must focus on the *analytical processes* used by these scholars, as well as the *basic assumptions* undergirding their analyses.

However, also as before, the historians discussed in this chapter—the conservative Sir Lewis Namier, liberals such as A. J. P. Taylor, William Newman (actually a political scientist with a strong historical orientation), and Charles A. Beard, and, representing radical scholarship, the authors of the official Soviet history of the war, as well as Lloyd

10. Christopher Thorne, *The Approach of War, 1938-1939* (London: Melbourne, 1967); Raymond J. Sontag, *A Broken World, 1919-1939* (New York: Harper and Row, 1971); William Carr, *Arms, Autarky and Aggression: A Study in German Foreign Policy, 1933-1939* (London: Edward Arnold, 1972); Norman Rich, *Hitler's War Aims: Ideology, the Nazi State, and the Course of Expansion* (New York: W. W. Norton, 1973); Klaus Hildebrand, *The Foreign Policy of the Third Reich* (Berkeley: University of California Press, 1973); Robert J. C. Butow, *Tojo and the Coming of the War* (Princeton: Princeton University Press, 1961); Dorothy Borg, *The United States and the Far Eastern Crisis of 1933-1938* (Cambridge, Mass.: Harvard University Press, 1964); Dorothy Borg and Shumpei Okamoto (eds.), *Pearl Harbor as History: Japanese American Relations, 1931-1941* (New York: Columbia University Press, 1973); and Stephen E. Pelz, *Race to Pearl Harbor: The Failure of the Second London Naval Conference and the Onset of World War II* (Cambridge, Mass.: Harvard University Press, 1974).

Gardner, T. W. Mason, and Klaus Hildebrand—have been selected not only because they "fit" the theoretical categories outlined in the first three chapters but also because they are significant in their own right. Indeed, our foremost criterion for selection has been their reputation as leading students of World War II.

What we offer here, it should be emphasized, is by no means an exhaustive account of existing World War II historiography. Others have done that elsewhere. Our presentation is designed to elicit from outstanding historians of the subject their ideological premises and analytical strategies. The result, we hope, is to demonstrate the usefulness of our interpretive framework for understanding the explanations of this major event.

The Conservative Tradition and World War II Historiography: Sir Lewis Namier

While there are few interpretations of the origins of World War II that can be called truly conservative, the tenets of that ideology are present to a great extent in the writings about the war of Sir Lewis Namier (1888-1960), one of the dominant figures of British historiography and one of the leading spokesmen for the orthodox interpretation of the conflict. Namier's volumes about World War II are important for our purposes because, in demonstrating the extent to which the orthodox/revisionist categories obscure the ideological factor, they reveal a major limitation of the prevailing interpretive framework.

Born in Poland, Namier was to be a most unusual Englishman. His family had been Jewish, but his father converted to Christianity and provided his son with the characteristic education of a Roman Catholic Polish gentleman. Yet because he was originally a Jew, Namier was never fully accepted by the Polish gentry. Leaving Poland as a young man, Namier spent some time in Vienna and Lausanne, arriving in England in 1908, where he studied first at the London School of Economics and then at Oxford University. Although he became a British citizen in 1913, it would be a mistake to underestimate the continuing influence of his Polish and, more importantly, Jewish heritage. Namier's subsequent attitude toward Germany, for example, was very much colored by these national and religious commitments. In fact, when Polish Jews experienced increasing oppression after Poland regained her independence, Namier renounced his upbringing and became an ardent Zionist. During World War I he served in the political intelligence department of the British Foreign Office. Following the war he taught briefly at Oxford and then launched a successful business career as a representative of British corporations in Austria and the United States. During the 1920s, as a private scholar, he returned once again to earlier researches on the imperial problem during the American Revolution. Finally, at the age of forty, he published his first book, the work for which he is primarily known: *The Structure of Politics at the Accession of George III* (1929), a microscopic examination of the workings of the English political system in the eighteenth century. This was followed immediately by a sequel, *England in the Age of the American Revolution* (1930). These two works reveal Namier's esteem for the stable society of upper-class England in the eighteenth century, and were also instrumental in his appointment, in 1931, to the chair of modern history at the University of Manchester, a position he held until 1953. During the 1930s he became deeply interested in the international diplomacy of that decade, and eventually produced the three books and numerous articles that most concern us here.[11]

Like Winston Churchill, Namier belonged to what D. C.

11. See Namier, *Diplomatic Prelude, 1938-1939*; *Europe in Decay, 1936-1940* (both cited above); and Namier, *In the Nazi Era* (London: Macmillan, 1952). Also see a series of essays first published in 1942 and then reissued in 1969, *Conflicts: Studies in Contemporary History* (New York: Books for Libraries Press, 1969). For biographical information, see the perceptive article by Henry R. Winkler, "Sir Lewis Namier," *Journal of Modern History*, 35 (March 1963), pp. 1-19.

Watt has called "the right-wing patriotic-chauvinist Germanophobe realist" school that strongly opposed appeasement.[12] For Namier the cause of World War II was clear and simple: German aggression. His major concern, therefore, was in determing whether Great Britain, France, and the Soviet Union could have prevented this aggression. The answer for Namier was unmistakably yes, and for him their pathetic inability to do so derived from "a failure of European statesmanship." In *Diplomatic Prelude, 1938-1939* (1948), a study of international relations from Munich to the German invasion of Poland, Namier rendered a stern judgment on British and French diplomacy regarding Germany:

It is difficult to fix or define the uneasy, fleeting, contradictory ideas entertained or professed at that time by French and British appeasers: there was embarrassment, desire for peace, purposeful credulity, an attempt on their part to recover their bearings and to reassert their self-respect . . . and, above all, exasperation with anyone who would try to probe that mass of emotional pretense and questionable reasoning. . . . Self-condemned to argue the justice of Hitler's conquests and to profess trust in his promises, they burdened their policy with make-believe and disabled themselves from striking out on a new and clear line.[13]

These conclusions were reinforced in his later work, *Europe in Decay* (1950), which focused on the failures of Western diplomacy from the occupation of the Rhineland to the fall of France.

Significantly, Namier's extensive analyses of the causes of World War II were formulated during a difficult period for him. A superb biography by his second wife, Julia, whom he married in 1947, provides many extremely penetrating, and occasionally painful, insights into Namier's personal life in the 1940s. A reflective, restive, and deeply troubled man who had earlier undergone psychoanalysis, Namier in those years "continued to slip steeply into misanthropy," wonder-

12. D. C. Watt, "Appeasement, the Rise of a Revisionist School?" p. 196.
13. Namier, *Diplomatic Prelude*, p. xi. See also Namier's "The Makers of Munich," in his *In the Nazi Era*, pp. 149-167.

ing "if it was not opportune to accept personal insanity as normal in a world he saw slipping into a nightmare." In 1945, shortly after deciding to divorce his first wife, Clara, from whom he had long been separated, and to terminate a six-year-long relationship with another woman, Namier had been dealt a devastating blow when Clara suddenly died of cancer. Racked with guilt and remorse, he returned to his teaching duties at the University of Manchester, according to Julia Namier's recollection, "in a condition of sombre self-hate bordering on a nervous breakdown." These paroxysms of self-contempt were alleviated only by frenetic work that consumed Namier's time and energy, resulting in the completion of three books and several essays. "Seen in the full context of his life," observes Julia Namier, "the three books written between 1940 and 1951 are the summary of a lifetime's observations transfused with close thought and based on a vast output of official and personal records going back to 1915 at least."[14]

Namier's unwavering opposition to the "policy of concessions" in the 1930s flowed naturally from his passionately anti-German sentiments. Nazism, in his opinion, was deeply rooted in the German nature: "With the Germans savagery is deliberately inculcated." In negatively contrasting the German "national character" with that of the British, Namier stressed the influence of religious Puritanism upon the latter. The Puritans, he argued in an essay written in 1941, insisted on men living in communities, believing as they did "that the control and corrective of the group was necessary to maintain the highest moral standards in the individual."[15]

14. Julia Namier, *Lewis Namier: A Biography* (London: Oxford University Press, 1971), pp. 258, 286. Especially useful in understanding the tormented condition of Namier's mind and his mounting physical disabilities as he was researching and writing these works are Chapters 14 ("Agonizing Reappraisals, 1940-1945") and 15 ("Hindered Recovery, 1946-1949").

15. See "Germany: National Character," an essay written for *The Spectator* (February 28, 1941) and reprinted in *Conflicts: Studies in Contemporary History*, pp. 79-80.

In lacking these high moral standards, Germans were easy prey for a demagogue such as Hitler. "Hitler understood the German people," concluded Namier, "which has found its full self-expression under his leadership. In this sense it is right to identify Hitler, the Nazis, and the German nation." The international conflict could justifiably be called "Hitler's War."[16]

This emphasis on the importance of community in molding a nation with moral principles was coupled with a recognition of another conservative tenet: the importance of hierarchical authority. One of the greatest virtues of British democracy, according to Namier, was that "respect for social superiority has prevented equality from ever being complete." "Liberty, in its very nature," he explained, "is an aristocratic or oligarchic attribute, possessed by single trees spreading above a lawn rather than by trees in a forest." Thus, for him, respect for prescriptive rights and social superiority formed the basis of British freedom and national strength.[17] The British are singularly blessed, this adopted son seemed to be saying, having been granted by history a special dispensation that enables them to cope with human nature better than most.

These notions about the importance of hierarchy and experienced leadership carried over into Namier's explanations for the coming of World War II, leading him to view international relations after 1918 in terms of a necessary dominance by the English-speaking nations. He wrote, for example, of the need for "an Anglo-Saxon world police" to make the League of Nations and United Nations work, and of the manner in which Great Britain must serve as "the advanced European bastion" in a powerful system of defense designed to keep Germany and other potential aggres-

16. See "Names and Realities," an essay written for *Time and Tide* (May 17, 1941) and reprinted in *Conflicts: Studies in Contemporary History*, p. 85.

17. See the essay "Democracy," written in March 1941 and reprinted in *Conflicts: Studies in Contemporary History*, p. 186-196.

sors in check. Lamenting the "missed opportunities" during the Weimar period for reintegrating a democratic Germany into the European system of nations, Namier in his last major work on the war, *In the Nazi Era* (1952), grew increasingly despondent and even suicidal over prospects for the future.[18]

Namier's analytical scheme, it should be pointed out, never acknowledged the significance of ideas and logic in directing human behavior: "The subject matter of history is human affairs, men in action, things which have happened and how they happened," he wrote near the end of his career. The events of history are "as complex and diversified as the men who wrought them, those rational beings whose knowledge is seldom sufficient, whose ideas are but distantly related to reality, and who are never moved by reason alone."[19] For Namier, as Henry Winkler has suggested, "unconscious promptings, atavistic memories and ingrained habits, combined with rational thought in conditioning men's behavior."[20] Curiously, Namier had a certain contept for his fellow conservative, Edmund Burke, because of the emphasis placed by Burke on the importance of party ideologies in the political world of 1760. To the contrary, writes Winkler, Namier was attracted to eighteenth-century society "precisely because it was the last period in which the ruling class had been able to engage in the rational pursuit of power in an ordered and static society, free from the fanaticism of ideas which marked the subsequent era of liberalism."[21] For him the twentieth century was a world embroiled in violence because it had lost its natural hierarchy (both national and international), its communal traditions, and its moral standards.

18. See *In the Nazi Era*, pp. 3-12.
19. Namier, *Avenues of History* (London: H. Hamilton, 1952), p. 1.
20. Winkler, "Sir Lewis Namier," p. 18.
21. *Ibid.*, p. 19.

*The Liberal Tradition and World War II
Historiography: A. J. P. Taylor, William J. Newman,
and Charles A. Beard*

Before beginning our discussion of liberal scholars of World War II, we would remind our readers that liberal ideology is characterized, among other ways, by an emphasis on the importance of individual personality and the exercise of reason, and, in most instances, by a commitment to capitalism as that system most likely to ensure freedom and democracy. We would also reiterate that there are three basic liberal theories of war: social-psychological, structural-functional, and group conflict.

The Social-Psychological Interpretation: A. J. P. Taylor. Until the appearance in 1961 of A. J. P. Taylor's sensational book, *The Origins of the Second World War*, historians generally endorsed the harsh indictment of Germany as responsible for that war advanced by such scholars as Sir Lewis Namier. Indeed, in most quarters the orthodox historians' case against Hitler and Germany was considered irrefutable. After 1961, the reasoning and conclusions of Taylor served as a catalyst for a thorough reappraisal of this traditional view, a reappraisal that continues today.

Born in 1906 in Lancashire, Taylor was the son of a prosperous Radical-Liberal cotton manufacturer. He attended a Quaker school in York before moving on to Oriel College, Oxford. After obtaining a degree in history (with First Class Honors), he studied diplomatic history in Vienna, and then served as a lecturer at the University of Manchester from 1930 to 1938. There he first met Sir Lewis Namier, who remained an important influence on his views about history and politics, although the two men had very different notions regarding the causes of World War II. Since the 1940s Taylor has been a Tutor and Fellow of Magdalen College at Oxford University.

When *The Origins of the Second World War* was published, Taylor was perhaps the best known and most popu-

lar of contemporary British historians. His previous historical works, like *The Course of German History* (1946) and
The Struggle for Mastery in Europe, 1848-1918 (1954), had
clearly established his scholarly reputation, at the same time
revealing his strong dislike for German leaders and their
policies, particularly in the Nazi period.[22] Furthermore, his
own involvement with British left wing activities, including
the Labour Party and the disarmament movement, made it
virtually impossible for anyone legitimately to accuse him of
pro-Fascist sympathies. Finally, his reputation was by no
means limited to academic circles, as his columns in the
Sunday Express and his appearances on the lecture circuit,
radio, and television provided a wide audience for his
opinions on numerous topics.

These features of Taylor's career help explain the ex-
plosive impact, especially in Great Britain, of his book on
the causes of World War II. How was it possible for a
scholar of his background and accomplishments to reach
conclusions so radically divergent from the accepted accounts of Hitler and Nazi foreign policy? Had the corrosive
acids of popularity seriously eroded his historical judgment?
Had success dulled his concern for the moral factor in human
behavior? Or had he simply succumbed to publicity-seeking
sensationalism?

These questions, and many others equally piercing, were
immediately posed by Taylor's critics.[23] What especially

22. A. J. P. Taylor, *The Course of German History* (London: H.
Hamilton, 1946); Taylor, *The Struggle for Mastery in Europe, 1848-1918*
(Oxford: Clarendon Press, 1954).

23. Among many reviews, see F. H. Hinsley, *Historical Journal*, 4
(1961), pp. 222-229; Alfred Cobban in *History*, 45 (October 1961), pp. 212-
217; A. L. Rowse, *New York Review of Books* (January 7, 1962), p. 6; G. F.
Hudson, *Commentary*, 33 (February 1962), pp. 178-184; Robert Spencer,
Canadian Historical Review, 43 (June 1962), pp. 136-144; and T. W.
Mason, "Some Origins of the Second World War," *Past and Present*, 29
(December 1964), pp 67-87. More supportive of Taylor's interpretation was
Harry Elmer Barnes, "A. J. P. Taylor and the Causes of World War II,"
New Individualist Review, 2 (Spring 1962), pp. 3-16. Also see the excellent
collection of reviews compiled by Wm. Rogers Louis (ed.), *The Origins of*

distressed many reviewers, in addition to his alleged misrepresentation of the historical record, was the enthusiastic acclaim accorded Taylor's book in right wing circles. The book was well received, for example, in the neo-Nazi organ *Reichsruf* and in the *Nation-Europa* (published by an ex-S.S. major), as well as in Sir Oswald Mosley's Fascist *Action*.[24]

The fact that a left wing historian produced a work applauded by the right wing is certainly not unprecedented. But it does render our task of ideological and theoretical classification all the more puzzling in Taylor's case. So does Taylor's continuing tendency to shift his perspectives, for, as a reviewer of his most recent work (*The Second World War: An Illustrated History*) points out, "The landscape [of World War II] looks different to Professor Taylor every time he traverses it."[25] Moreover, Taylor has elsewhere made clear his disdain for the use of theory in the writing of history:

Most historians start with the assumption that Hitler was an indescribably wicked man who was set on world war for some reason or other. Then they construct a perfectly plausible book about war origins, based on this assumption. Hoggan started with the opposite assumption that Hitler was a man of peace and that Halifax was the deliberate planner of war. On this basis, he also constructed a perfectly plausible book. I draw the moral that it is better to start without assumptions and try to construct a book based on the political and military events.[26]

the Second World War: A. J. P. Taylor and His Critics (New York: John Wiley, 1972); and W. H. Dray, "Concepts of Causation in A. J. P. Taylor's Account of the Origins of the Second World War," *History and Theory*, 2 (1978), pp. 149-174. We have also profited greatly from the special issue of *The Journal of Modern History*, 49 (March 1977), devoted to the work and historiography of Taylor.

24. See, for example, comments in Elizabeth Wiskemann's letter to *The Times Literary Supplement* (June 2, 1961), p. 361, and Cole, "Critics of the Taylor View of History," p. 154.

25. Neil Ascherson, "The Good War," *New York Review of Books* (January 22, 1976), p. 14.

26. Taylor, "War Origins Again," *Past and Present*, 30 (April 1965), p. 111.

This unequivocal declaration appears to confirm what another reviewer has noted: "Taylor himself has never made any comprehensive statement of why he writes history, or why anyone should write history at all."[27]

Be that as it may, the vital core of Taylor's book is the assertion that Hitler had no desire for European conquest or war from March 1933 to September 1939. In truth, says Taylor, the Führer's fundamental goal was simply to revise the unjust Treaty of Versailles and thereby restore Germany's "natural" position in Europe. Even in the most extreme case, all Hitler required to achieve this end was that Austria, Czechoslovakia, and perhaps the Balkan states should become economic and political satellites of Germany (as all but Austria are today of Russia). Germany was in no way equipped to conquer all of Europe, even if Hitler had wanted to. "The state of German rearmament in 1939," Taylor contends, "gives the decisive proof that Hitler was not contemplating general war, and probably not intending war at all."[28] World War II, then, "far from being premeditated, was a mistake, the result on both sides of diplomatic blunders."[29] If we wish to locate the true origins of World War II, in Taylor's opinion, we must go back to the 1914-1919 period: "If one asks the rather crude question, 'what was the war about?', the answer for the first [world war] is: 'to decide how Europe should be remade', but for the second [world war] merely: 'to decide whether this remade Europe should continue.' The first war explains the second and, in fact, caused it, in so far as one event causes another."[30]

Thus Taylor's heroes (although he would be reluctant to use that term) are those European statesmen—above all, Ramsay MacDonald and Neville Chamberlain—who ap-

27. Edward B. Segel, "A. J. P. Taylor and History," *The Review of Politics*, 26 (October 1964), pp. 531-546, and reprinted in Wm. Roger Louis (ed.), *The Origins of the Second World War*, p. 13.

28. Taylor, *The Origins of the Second World War*, p. 211.

29. *Ibid.*, p. 212.   30. *Ibid.*, p. 23.

preciated the reasonableness of Germany's desire to undo the effects of World War I. Chamberlain, motivated not by fear of Germany's power but by a realistic hope for the general pacification of Europe, assumed with good reason that Hitler would be satisfied with a series of concessions willingly made. And the Munich Conference of September 29-30, 1938, far from constituting a cowardly betrayal of principle and a diplomatic disaster for Britain, was actually "a triumph for those who had preached equal justice between peoples; a triumph for those who had courageously denounced the harshness and shortsightedness of Versailles."[31]

As we can see even from this brief account, Taylor's causal explanation for World War II combines a particular *objective situation* (the failure of the Allies to divide Germany up before concluding a punitive peace in 1919) with a series of *human blunders* in the late 1930s (especially by British war advocates, among them both Conservatives and Labourites). The Allies' earlier mistake created the "historical necessity" for Germany's attempt to restore her "natural" pre-World War I position. From 1919 onward, therefore, intelligent European statesmen—such as Hitler and Chamberlain —could only acknowledge this historical necessity and try to act accordingly. Unfortunately, however, human intelligence did not prevail in the 1930s. But, Taylor would argue, it seldom does.

For Taylor, then, human frailty and error, not human aggressiveness, are what so often prevent the intelligent recognition of historical realities.[32] Hitler's role as described by Taylor—namely, that of a leader pulled along to a great extent by events over which he had little control—is thus an essential element of Taylor's own implicit "theory of history." One critic, drawing upon statements in *The Origins of*

31. *Ibid.*, p. 184.

32. *Ibid.*, p. 209. Taylor writes: "Of course Hitler's nature and habits played their part. It was easy for him to threaten, and hard for him to conciliate. This is far from saying that he foresaw, or deliberately projected, the European dominance which he seemed to achieved in 1942. All statesmen aim to win. The size of the winnings often surprises them."

the Second World War, has offered a metaphorical description of Taylor's "non-philosophy of history":

The Second World War was as little due to National Socialist theory as road accidents are due to the existence of cars and roads. Accidents are not the result of the driver's intent, but to poor handling and conditions outside his control. The Nazis did not intend war: it came about through mistakes and chance events. Wars, like road accidents, are the result of human mistakes and to affix guilt would be to argue that man controls history.[33]

Or consider Taylor's own comment on his view of historical forces: "Certainly the development of history has its own logical laws. But these laws resemble rather those by which flood-water flows into hitherto unseen channels and forces itself finally to an unpredictable sea."[34]

These various observations are useful as we attempt to classify Taylor according to the ideological traditions and theoretical categories presented in the first three chapters of this book. Most readily apparent is that, despite his left-of-center political activities, Taylor's historical explanation for the origins of World War II is certainly not radical. In fact, in Chapter 10 of his book and in a later article, he firmly rejects a Marxist analysis based on a crisis of overproduction resulting from Germany's industrial recovery, thereby requiring an expansionist foreign policy: "There is little evidence for this dogma."[35] More recently, in perhaps the most extensive and revealing personal account of his version of history, Taylor clearly separates himself from Marxism:

33. Cole, "Critics of the Taylor View of History," p. 143. In his later article, "War Origins Again," p. 113, Taylor reasserted his position on Hitler: "Hitler was treading, rather cautiously, in Bethmann's footsteps. There was nothing new or unusual in his aims and outlook. His methods were often new. He was a gambler in foreign, as in home, affairs; a skillful tactician, waiting to exploit the opportunities which others offered him. His easy successes made him careless, as was not surprising, and he gambled steadily higher. He found the path of violence increasingly attractive and the path of negotiation increasingly tedious. But essentially his stake, if I may for once allude to profound forces, lay in the logic of the German problem."

34. Quoted in Segel, "A. J. P. Taylor and History," p. 15.

35. Taylor, *The Origins of the Second World War*, pp. 209-210.

I called myself a Marxist from the time I became a Socialist. But, reading more history at Oxford, I began to feel that Marxism did not work. Consider the famous sentence in the Communist Manifesto: "The history of all hitherto recorded society is the history of class struggles." Very impressive but not true. Perhaps all history ought to have been the history of class struggles, but things did not work out that way. There have been long periods of class collaboration and many struggles that were not about class at all. I suppose my mind is too anarchic to be fitted into any system of thought. Like Johnson's friend Edwards, I, too, tried to be a Marxist but common sense kept breaking in.[36]

Moreover, there is much about Taylor's accounts that sounds quite conservative. As. D. C. Watt has pointed out, Taylor "sees relations between states as taking place in a Hobbesian state of nature restrained not so much by rules and conventions as by the 'perpetual quadrille of the Balance of Power', the product of the mutual jealously of the great powers."[37] We must also note Taylor's stress on human weakness and frailty, his views of man's inability to control history, and his rejection of the historical role of ideas.

Nevertheless, in the final analysis, it is clear that Taylor's explanatory model is built primarily upon liberal, social-psychological assumptions. Taylor allows this fact to be established again and again. He refers to Mussolini as being "deluded" about the strength of Italy, argues that until 1936 "French statesmen continued to believe that they could lay down the law throughout Europe," and points out that even after the German reoccupation of the Rhineland "French statesmen, and British ones also, believed that France herself was impregnable." Concluding that victory in World War II marked the virtual end of the British Empire, Taylor asserts that Churchill's belief that Great Britain would survive as a major power "appears in retrospect as fantastic as Mussolini's belief that Italy would become one." "For

36. Taylor, "Accident Prone, or What Happened Next," *Journal of Modern History*, 49 (March 1977), p. 4.
37. D. C. Watt, "Some Aspects of A. J. P. Taylor's Work as Diplomatic Historian," *Journal of Modern History*, 49 (March 1977), p. 24.

that matter," Taylor continues, "Hitler, too, dreamed impossible dreams when he supposed that Germany would contend with Soviet Russia and the United States for mastery of the world." "After the war Europe's age was over," he concludes, "and the Second World War only made clear what was happening. Mussolini was no more mistaken than other European statesmen. He merely displayed his mistake more blatantly."[38]

Thus Taylor, in *The Origins of the Second World War* and in subsequent writings, ultimately has recourse to cognitive processes to explain the causes of war. What was really wrong, according to him, was that major policy-makers acted on false assumptions and were guided by faulty perceptions of their own nations and of other nations. These distorted images—Churchill's of Britain and France, Hitler's of Soviet Russia and the United States, Mussolini's of Italy—shaped their individual adjustments to reality and led eventually to international conflict. Taylor is arguing that while conscious decisions of particular individuals can profoundly affect the course of events, they can only bring on difficulty and violence when they are made in ignorance of basic geopolitical forces.

Taylor, to be sure, is correctly identified in political terms as being "on the Left." Yet he is certainly not analytically radical when he refuses to be concerned with increasing our understanding of the totality of economic, social, and political developments, and chooses instead to focus narrowly on high-level decision-makers in the political structure and on the distribution of political power among various nation-states. "In this way," Edward Segel points out in a fair-minded account of Taylor's historical philosophy, "economic, cultural, and social developments are often passed over with a minimum of treatment, unless they seem to Taylor to have some noticeable effect on the power relation-

38. See Taylor's review of Denis Mack Smith, *Mussolini's Roman Empire* (New York: Viking Press, 1976) in the *New York Review of Books* (August 5, 1976), pp. 3-4.

ships of the major characters of his drama."[39] Indeed, we must affirm that Taylor's conception of the balance of power on occasion resembles the hierarchical premises of conservatives more than the pluralistic notions of many liberal scholars. This is particularly true when he deals with the problems of Germany, a nation that he alternately respects as the strongest power of Europe and fears as militaristic oppressor of the continent.[40]

Still, the essential liberalism of this eclectic and flamboyant historian will not be denied. In the end we find him contending for a balance of power that allows Germany to be the leader but not the master of the situation. On the day that European statesmen and peoples, both German and Allied, can bring themselves to perceive accurately the necessity of this, Taylor implies, on that day Europe will have peace.

The Structural-Functional Interpretation: William J. Newman. As we have seen in Chapter 2, a systems approach is used by structural-functionalists to understand the operation of both domestic and international affairs. In that chapter we briefly described the views of the leading structural-functionalist, Talcott Parsons, who defines a social system (in somewhat complicated terminology) as "the interaction of a plurality of actors, in which the action is oriented by rules which are complexes of complementary expectations concerning roles and sanctions."[41] The major problem of any social system, according to this perspective, is to achieve and maintain an ordered equilibrium. Thus structural-functional theory examines those values and procedures that relate to a given system's ability to maintain an equilibrium and to respond to changes within its environment.[42]

39. Segel, "A. J. P. Taylor and History," p. 16.

40. See Taylor, *The Struggle for Mastery in Europe*, pp. 567-568.

41. Talcott Parsons and Edward A. Shils (eds.), *Toward a General Theory of Action* (New York: Harper and Row, 1962), p. 195.

42. See Chapter 4 of James E. Dougherty and Robert L. Pfaltzgraff, Jr.,

156   HISTORIANS AND WORLD WAR II

Unfortunately for our immediate purposes here, there have been few explicit, detailed applications of structural-functional theory to the historical example of World War II. Most of the empirical research done on international relations from this perspective has dealt with patterns of communication or with the integration of trans-national communities.[43] Thus the book selected for discussion in this section—William J. Newman's *The Balance of Power in the Interwar Years, 1919-1939* (1968)— is in some ways unsatisfactory, for one will find no mention in this work of Parsons, Karl Deutsch, David Easton, or any other structural-functionalist.[44] In fact, the book appears to exist in a theoretical void. Yet, as we shall see, Newman's fundamental assumptions are quite consistent with those of structural-functional theory, and his book therefore serves as a reasonably good example of the application of this perspective to an understanding of the causes of World War II.

Newman (1919-   ), a specialist in international relations and American foreign policy who teaches at Boston University, attempts in his book to merge the disciplines of history and political science, believing, contrary to A. J. P. Taylor, that "there is need for bringing theory into some viable relationship to reality."[45] Again unlike Taylor, who stri-

Contending Theories of International Relations (Philadelphia and New York: G. Braziller, 1961) and *Liberalism and the Retreat from Politics* (New York: J.B. Lippincott, 1971), pp. 102-137. Also see David Easton, *A Systems Analysis of Political Life* (New York: John Wiley and Sons, 1965), pp. 284-285, 484-488; Easton, *A Framework for Political Analysis* (Englewood Cliffs, N.J.: Prentice-Hall, 1965); and Herbert J. Spiro, *World Politics: The Global System (Homewood, Ill.: Dorsey Press, 1966).*

43. See, for example, Bruce Russett, *Community and Contention: Britain and America in the Twentieth Century* (Cambridge, Mass.: M.I.T. Press, 1963); and Philip Jacob and James Toscano (eds.), *The Integration of Political Communities* (Philadelphia: J. B. Lippincott, 1964).

44. William J. Newman, *The Balance of Power in the Interwar Years, 1919-1939* (New York: Random House, 1968).

45. *Ibid.,* p. vii. This Newman should not be confused with historian William L. Neumann, author of *Making the Peace, 1941-1945* (Washington D.C.: Foundation for Foreign Affairs, 1950) and *After Victory* (New York, 1967). Newman is also the author of *The Futilitarian Society* (New York: G. Braziller, 1961) and *Liberalism and the Retreat from Politics* (New

dently maintains that Nazi foreign policy was simply a restatement of the old "German problem," Newman views the 1930s as "a unique phenomenon bounded by the existence of Nazism." "There has never been anything quite like Hitler and his foul gang," he contends, arguing further that Hitler's death terminated "a special experience."[46]

Despite his notions about the unprecedented and special character of Hitler and the Nazis, however, Newman urges us *not* to concentrate on the leading personalities of the period, "since individuals participate in international relations mainly through the internal political systems of independent and separate states."[47] The basic question posed by that era, in Newman's view, is not the intentions of Adolf Hitler, or of any other European statesman, for that matter. Rather, it is whether (1) the style of German foreign policy in the 1930s will be emulated in the future by other states, and (2) the system-oriented states have learned how to cope with and compel modification in such tactics as Germany used.[48]

Newman argues that the most important task for international relations in the 1930s was to convert Hitler and the Nazi leaders to a "system of brokerage." Such a system of give-and-take, in which demands would not only be made but also accepted, would have provided (as it had so often in the past) a means of communication among states permitting both tacit and explicit agreement about the distribution of power.[49] Had Newman chosen to use the language of structural-functionalism, he might well have defined this system of brokerage as "a system of interaction among participants in international politics governed by rules that provide for complementary expectations concerning roles and sanctions." The point is that while Newman's language is less complicated than Parsons' and other structural-

---

York: G. Braziller, 1964), and is presently working on a book on American attitudes towards globalism centering on the World War II years.

46. Newman, *The Balance of Power in the Interwar Years*, p. 33.
47. *Ibid.*, p. 64.   48. *Ibid.*, p. 34.   49. *Ibid.*, pp. 38-43, 69-74.

functionalists, his assumptions and explanatory categories are virtually identical.

Discovering the precise combination of coercion and appeasement needed to bring Hitler into line was crucial, Newman contends, lest the delicate balance of power system established by France, Britain, and Germany in the Locarno Pact of 1925 be destroyed. In the 1930s, the all-important task of "brokering" Hitler and Germany into the balance of power system fell primarily to Neville Chamberlain and other British leaders intimately involved with both the domestic and international systems. The central events in their lack of success were three: the German reoccupation of the Rhineland in 1936, the seizure of Austria in 1938, and the occupation of Sudetenland in 1938. These were central because after 1938-1939 the increasingly even balance of military power enabled Hitler to take greater risks and to become convinced finally that Germany could wage war to achieve its ends.

From Newman's implicit systems perspective, then, the decade of the 1930s constitutes a "special experience" because this overriding integrative goal dominated international relations, yet ultimately, due to the extreme recalcitrance of Hitler's Germany and the ineffectiveness of Germany's opponents, was never achieved. Regardless of the many obstacles, however, Newman believes that the attempt to convert Germany "to brokerage" could have worked, thereby establishing an integrated, coherently functioning international system. Why, then, did it fail?

In attempting to answer that question, Newman does not deny the social-psychological aspects of the failure of brokerage, noting, for example, Chamberlain's tragic misperception in 1938 in overestimating Germany's military strength. (In fact, Newman argues, Germany was in a position of *military inferiority* through 1940.) Furthermore, Newman endorses the widespread assumption that Hitler was allowed to pursue his aggressive policies because of the "ignorance" and "mental blindness" of the British and French. He thus clearly acknowledges the role of misperception and false images.

At the same time, however, Newman disagrees with A. J. P. Taylor in stressing how unusually shrewd Hitler was, as the Nazi leader sought to manipulate the major European nation-states so that their superior military power could not be directed against Germany. From Newman's perspective, what was particularly insidious is that Hitler consistently played a "pseudobroker role," unwilling to assume the role of a true broker who would mediate between the demands of his own state and those of other states. "But he did play *at* the part," writes Newman, "imitating the role without ever acting out its substance."[50] The irony is that had Hitler adopted the brokerage role (as Stresemann might have done), Germany would have gained many of its basic aims without resort to war. But it is precisely because Hitler rejected the framework of the balance of power that he refused to play the broker's role. This stance enabled him to undermine the balance of power while pretending merely to modify it.

In *The Balance of Power in the Interwar Years* Hitler is presented as the complete opposite of a broker. Instead, he is viewed as a "risktaker," a "totalitarian outlaw" who worked to destroy the balance of power as a system. "The risktaker," according to Newman, "rejects the idea of restraint on the part of the members of an international system and the whole idea of the balance of power."[51] Because brokerage was rejected, the probability of forceful military solutions was greatly increased. And the integrative potentialities of international relations, so important to structural-functionalists, were thereby completely denied.

Still, in failing to react imaginatively and perceptively to the unusual challenge, the British and French must also bear considerable responsibility for the collapse of the international system in the 1930s. Neither country was able to generate a timely and proper combination of the carrot and

50. *Ibid.*, p. 156.   51. *Ibid.*, p. 158.

the stick, a combination that would have required an appeal to mutual values as well as an empathy to needs and the threat of force. It was not, as A. J. P. Taylor might contend, that Germany had been thrust from its natural dominance in 1919 and must be allowed to reclaim it. It was rather that the system needed to be fortified through compromise and firmness.

At the last, then, Newman's analysis shifts the blame from human blunders or the wickedness of individuals and groups and places it on the difficulty of maintaining a balance under such circumstances. To use the terminology of the structural-functional theorists, the system was unable to maintain integration and equilibrium, and to respond creatively to changes within its environment. "The struggle for the balance of power requires the constant invention of new policies," Newman reminds us. In such statements he reveals himself as a much more optimistic structural-functionalist than Woodrow Wilson or G. Lowes Dickinson, for whom continuing international integration requires international organization.

The Group Conflict Interpretation: Charles A. Beard. No assessment of the theoretical assumptions of World War II historiography would be complete without a discussion of the works of Charles A. Beard (1874-1948). Author or co-author of 33 books, 14 texts, and scores of articles and reviews, Beard is best known for his controversial work, *An Economic Interpretation of the Constitution of the United States* (1913). Less well known is Beard's interest in American foreign policy and the causes of war. His writings in this field provoked additional controversy and are the focus of our attention here.

A persistent theme in Beard's writings is the close relationship between economic motives and political behavior in the formulation of both domestic and foreign policies. Consistently until the mid-1930s, and inconsistently thereafter, Beard was concerned with the political significance of private property. Indeed, his emphasis on conflicts and struggles among interests and classes has led some observers to conclude that Beard's underlying assumptions were Marxist.[52] We do know that the Marxist tradition was important to Beard. He was introduced to the writings of Marx as an undergraduate at DePauw in the late 1890s. Later, as a graduate student at Oxford, he came into contact with radicals in the British trade unions and the Fabian Society. Socialist writers such as A. M. Simons and Gustavus Myers also exercised an influence on Beard in his intellectually formative years.

Despite periodic flirtations with radicalism and radical theory, however, Beard never developed a firm commitment to Marxist analysis or a systematic theory of imperialism. "His essential grievance," observed Richard Hofstadter, "was not against a class, nor even the property system as such, but against the *waste* of energies entailed by modern competitive organization."[53] "The outstanding feature of Beard's brand of economic interpretation of politics, whether in 1913 or in 1934," writes Gerald Stourzh,

was its un-Marxian stress, implicit or explicit, on the economic *motives* of individuals or groups. This insinuation of the acquisitive instinct as the most crucial attribute of human nature lies at the very bottom of Beard's incapacity to take into account the genuinely political aspects of foreign policy.[54]

52. See, for example, Morton White, *Social Thought in America: The Revolt Against Formalism* (New York: Viking Press, 1949), p. 43.

53. Richard Hofstadter, *The Progressive Historians: Turner, Beard, Parrington* (New York: Alfred A. Knopf, 1968), p. 175.

54. Gerald Stourzh, "Charles A. Beard's Interpretation of American Foreign Policy," *World Affairs Quarterly*, 28 (July 1957), p. 126. Also see Bernard C. Borning, *The Political and Social Thought of Charles A. Beard* (Seattle: University of Washington Press, 1962), pp. 87-88, 160-161, 198 (n. 57). Arthur A. Ekirch, Jr., has recently reached the same conclusion in "Charles A. Beard and Reinhold Niebuhr: Contrasting Conceptions of National Interest in American Foreign Policy," *Mid-America*, 59 (April-July 1977), p. 106: "Not a systematic political theorist, and more profoundly influenced by American history than by international socialist thinkers like Marx, Beard, as Max Lerner later noted, 'was horrified by the Communist state and its values, and he never showed much interest even in a commitment to democratic socialism.'"

A careful examination of Beard's major works, then, reveals not so much a Marxist belief in the importance of class struggle as it does a liberal attempt to explain the role of dynamic groups. To be sure, Beard worked more within the "dualistic" tradition of the progressive school of historiography (the perpetual struggle of "the people" against "the interests") than the "pluralistic" version enunciated in the eighteenth century by James Madison in *The Federalist* (Number 10). But as we shall see, both as scholar and as activist Beard remained a liberal reformer, not a socialist revolutionary.

Beard's liberalism may be discerned in his understanding of the nature of imperialism. His initial thoughts on this subject were stimulated at the turn of the century by the territorial acquisitions of the United States in the Pacific and the Caribbean. It was possible, Beard observed in 1901, that imperialism might have constructive consequences. "Imperialism is the world-creating process," he explained. If this process were wrong, "then history since the beginning of time, and especially since the beginning of the seventeenth century, has been wrong, a mistake to be deplored."[55] Beard was therefore not critical of imperialism *as a system* but only of those individuals and groups that pursued excessive self-aggrandizement as part of the relationship. These were the persons preventing imperialism from achieving beneficial results. In his numerous subsequent books and articles, Beard never went much beyond a description of the way in which interest groups like bankers, financiers, arms manufacturers, and the various bureaucracies of the Army and Navy often self-consciously manipulate foreign policy for their own ends. Clearly, from Beard's viewpoint, imperialism was not an imperative of capitalism.[56]

55. Beard, "A Living Empire, I," *Young Oxford*, 3 (October 1901), pp. 24-25, as quoted in Thomas C. Kennedy, *Charles A. Beard and American Foreign Policy* (Gainesville: The University Presses of Florida, 1975), p. 9.

56. See Beard, *The Idea of National Interest* (New York, 1934). In a two-volume college text, *The Development of Modern Europe* (Boston: Ginn, 1907, 1908), written with his Columbia University colleague James

Beard continued to eschew radical analyses in his explanations of the origins of World War I when he explicitly repudiated the notion that it was "a capitalist war for colonies, markets, and concessions." In a series of lectures delivered at Dartmouth College in 1921, Beard rejected an explanation based on inexorable forces in favor of one that placed responsibility on specific individuals who freely reached wrong policy decisions. A few years later, in a personal letter to revisionist historian Harry Elmer Barnes, Beard reiterated that view: "I hesitate in measuring out the exact amount of damnation due to the liars and incompetents who got the world into the mess of 1914—but none of them can get too much."[57] And in a well-known textbook *The Rise of American Civilization* (1927), written with his wife Mary, Beard once again stressed the pressures of interest groups—investors, munitions makers, merchants, and manufacturers—in the coming of World War I.[58] By 1932, this concern about the role of dynamic groups had come to focus primarily upon the American military establishment, particularly the Navy. Throughout the 1930s Beard regarded increased naval appropriations as a serious threat to world peace and domestic recovery from the Depression.[59]

Harvey Robinson, Beard explained imperialism in terms of two powerful forces: factories seeking markets and capital seeking investments. This process necessitated large military and naval establishments, which in turn created a requirement for increased armaments. Not only did these developments increase the likelihood of war, but they also prevented nations from using those resources for socially beneficial purposes. At the same time, Beard hoped that international trade and finance might reduce international rivalries and thereby promote world peace. See Vol. 2, pp. 328, 366.

57. Beard to Barnes, July 14, 1926, Barnes Papers, Western History Research Center, University of Wyoming, cited in Kennedy, *Charles A. Beard and American Foreign Policy*, p. 46.

58. Charles and Mary Beard, *The Rise of American Civilization*, 2 vols. (New York: Macmillan, 1927), Vol. 2, pp. 630-631.

59. See, for example, Beard's *The Navy: Defense or Portent?* (New York: Harper and Bros., 1932), and concurrent articles in *The New Republic* and *Harper's* on the "Big Navy Boys." Also see Thomas C.

This accusatory approach to interest groups, while extremely unpopular in the 1920s, received a substantial boost in the mid-1930s with the publication of the Senate hearings of the Nye Committee. Beard, like many others, was deeply impressed by that committee's major conclusion: responsibility for United States entry into World War I rested squarely on the shoulders of international bankers and munitions makers—the so-called "merchants of death."[60] Nevertheless, while this conclusion provided support for Beard's earlier interpretation of United States involvement, he ultimately rejected it as overly simplistic. In *The Devil Theory of War* (1936), Beard argued that "wicked" politicians and "profit-crazed" bankers do not by themselves cause international wars. In focusing blame on individual scapegoats, the "devil theory" obscured the manner in which decision-makers are dependent upon their economic, political, and social environment: "War is not the work of a demon. It is our very own work, for which we prepare wittingly or not, in ways of peace." Politicians embody the will of their constituents just as bankers reflect the demands of the marketplace. Prior to World War I, more specifically, American prosperity was dependent upon a growing trade with the Allies. Woodrow Wilson *had* to take the United States to war abroad in order to avoid economic collapse at home. Politicians and business leaders, in short, do not operate in a vacuum. Their freedom of action is severely limited by material conditions and impersonal forces.[61]

Kennedy, "Charles A. Beard and the 'Big Navy Boys,'" *Military Affairs*, 31 (Summer 1967), pp. 65-73. For the important influence on Beard in the early 1930s and thereafter of the German historian Eckart Kehr (and his thesis regarding the "primacy of domestic politics"), see Arthur Lloyd Skop, "The Primacy of Domestic Politics: Eckart Kehr and the Intellectual Development of Charles A. Beard," *History and Theory*, 13 (1974), pp. 119-131.

60. On the Nye Committee, see John E. Wiltz, *In Search of Peace: The Senate Munitions Inquiry, 1934-1936* (Baton Rouge: Louisiana State University Press, 1963); and Manfred Jonas, *Isolationism in America, 1935-1941* (Ithaca, N.Y.: Cornell University Press, 1966), pp. 145-146.

61. Beard, *The Devil Theory of War: Inquiry Into the Nature of History*

Beard thus moved very close to a radical analysis in the first half of *The Devil Theory of War*, implying that involvement with the Allies had resulted from the need of American capitalism to obtain export markets. Yet is is important to note that having entered the theoretical terrain of radicalism, Beard quickly returned in that same book to the more familiar assumptions of a conspiratorial variant of liberal group conflict theory. While arguing fervently for sweeping mandatory neutrality laws designed to prevent involvement in Europe by the United States in the late 1930s, Beard frankly acknowledged the difficulty of enforcing such laws: "But enough of them can be so enforced," he was confident enough to predict, "as to prevent the bankers and politicians from guiding the nation into calamity as in 1914-1917."[62]

Here Beard, despite his argument earlier about the importance of "context" and of collective responsibility for a nation's involvement in war, ultimately endorses the very devil theory he had set out to disprove, or at least to amend.[63] He was reinforced in this endorsement by his growing distrust of President Franklin Roosevelt, itself intensified by his discovery of a most disturbing historical precedent: the secret activities of Woodrow Wilson, Colonel House, and Secretary of State Lansing on behalf of American business interests. The lesson derived by Beard from this experience was the absolute necessity of open public debate: "If we go to war, let us go to war for some grand national

---

and the Possibility of Keeping Out of War (New York: Vanguard Press, 1936), pp. 21-23, 29.

62. *Ibid.*, pp. 118-123.

63. See Jonas, *Isolationism in America*, p. 153: Beard's book "thus had the effect of advertising, rather than refuting, the devil theory." Also see Warren I. Cohen, *The American Revisionists: The Lessons of Intervention in World War I* (Chicago: University of Chicago Press, 1967), p. 18?; Hofstadter, *The Progressive Historians*, p. 332; and Kennedy, *Charles A. Beard and American Foreign Policy*, pp. 83-84. Ronald Radosh, in *Prophets on the Right: Profiles of Conservative Critics of American Globalism* (New York: Simon and Schuster, 1975), emphasizes Beard's radicalism.

and human advantage openly discussed and deliberately arrived at, and not to bail out farmers, bankers and capitalists or to save politicians from the pain of dealing with a domestic crisis."[64]

For the next decade, until his death in 1948, Beard resolutely pursued the consequences of President Roosevelt's inability to learn this same "lesson." By the late 1930s, completely dismayed by the failures of the New Deal's recovery program, Beard was advocating above all else the pressing need for domestic reform. International rivalries for world markets and unpublicized agreements by high-level decision-makers could only serve to hinder the achievement of that all-important goal. Even as Nazi troops were invading Poland in September 1939, Beard was composing a brief polemical essay entitled *Giddy Minds and Foreign Quarrels*, based on a passage from Shakespeare's *Henry IV* in which the dying King advises his son to keep the masses preoccupied with foreign adventures so as to divert their attention from domestic inequities. Beard's message seemed clear and unmistakable: a devious Franklin Delano Roosevelt, unable to master an incorrigible Depression, was trying to "solve" his problems by dragging the American people into a war against their will.[65]

One overriding theme dominates the remainder of Beard's writings on foreign policy: domestic considerations, not external developments, determine such policy. Abandoning one of the leading assumptions of *The Devil Theory of War*—namely, that "wicked men" do not make war by themselves—Beard proceeded to carry out a relentless search for domestic villains. That this search produced results is attested by his last two books—*American Foreign Policy in the Making, 1932-1940* (1946) and *President Roosevelt and the Coming of the War, 1941* (1948)—which constitute a massive indictment of a single "devil," Franklin D. Roosevelt, a President who publicly promised peace while pri-

64. Beard, *The Devil Theory of War*, pp. 123-124.
65. See Beard, *Giddy Minds and Foreign Quarrels: An Estimate of American Foreign Policy* (New York: Macmillan, 1939).

vately preparing for war. Clearly, then, Beard's own social theory had evolved in such a way as to justify an emphasis on personal responsibility in human affairs.

Beard's provocative views regarding United States entry into World War II have often been misrepresented or misunderstood by those who are deeply offended by his adamant isolationist position. In 1949, for example, Lewis Mumford accused him of becoming an abettor of "tyranny, sadism, and human defilement."[66] Several critics contended that his "single-minded vendetta" against Roosevelt destroyed any possibility of scholarly objectivity.[67] Some even suggested that Beard's mental capacities had been diminished by age. More relevant to our considerations here is the assertion by Richard Hofstadter that Beard's attitudes toward World War II pulled him "steadily toward the right, cutting him loose from his moorings in traditional American liberalism."[68]

Others, particularly after the Vietnam experience, have found much to praise in Beard's volumes. "It was not that his mind slowed down," suggests William Appleman Williams, "but rather that his heart speeded up." Williams urges us to pay attention to Beard's emphasis on the importance of moral integrity in public life: "For Beard did not oppose the war that was fought. He did oppose the way that Roosevelt led this country into war, and the New Deal's strong inclination to think it was America's job to reform the world."[69] And as Ronald Radosh has pointed out in a

66. See Lewis Mumford, "Mr. Beard and His 'Basic History.'" *Saturday Review* (December 2, 1944), p. 27.

67. See, for example, Samuel Eliot Morison, "Did Roosevelt Start the War? History Through a Beard," *Atlantic Monthly* (August 1948), p. 92.

68. Hofstadter, *The Progressive Historians*, p. 340.

69. William Appleman Williams, "Charles Austin Beard: The Intellectual as Tory-Radical," in Harvey Goldberg (ed.), *American Radicals: Some Problems and Personalities* (New York: Monthly Review Press, 1957), pp. 305, 306. Also see Williams, "A Note on Charles Austin Beard's Search for a General Theory of Causation," *American Historical Review*, 61 (October 1956), pp. 59-80. Beard had earlier warned against United States global Messianism in *The Open Door at Home: A Trial Philosophy of National Interest* (New York: Macmillan, 1934).

recent volume, "Beard did not concentrate on the evils of the Nazi system—he assumed most Americans did not want a fascist system—but on the disintegration of the institutions that made American democracy strong."[70] Unless Roosevelt's actions were vigorously and vocally challenged, Beard had warned, a future President "in a campaign for re-election may publicly promise the people to keep the country out of war and after victory at the polls, may set out secretly on a course designed or practically certain to bring war upon the country."[71]

Though Beard in his last works may have largely abandoned his earlier tendency to blame runaway interest groups for war (one could also argue that by narrowing his focus he was simply trying to make a point), he certainly did not, as Hofstadter claims, abandon liberalism for conservatism. Nor, of course, did Beard in his final years adopt a radical perspective on social conflict and war. He remained a liberal, thoroughly committed to pluralism and capitalism, as well as honesty in government. He also remained a reformer, and in a number of important ways—by arguing that war abroad is destructive to reform at home, by warning of the growth of an enormous military establishment, and by pointing to the dangers of executive usurpation of power—he anticipated much of the liberal and New Left critique of American democracy in the 1960s.

The Radical Tradition and World War II Historiography: The Soviet Version and the Social Democratic Alternative

Despite the predominance of liberal interpretations, the problem of the origins of World War II would appear to be highly susceptible to radical class analysis. After all, the world had recently experienced a severe, crippling Depression caused by the failure of the capitalist system. Class conflict in leading countries had intensified because of

70. Radosh, *Prophets on the Right*, p. 41.
71. Beard, *President Roosevelt and the Coming of the War*, p. 582.

increasing economic hardship. The Western capitalist nations had not been able to use the machinery of liberal internationalism to enforce the settlement of 1919. Given these potentially radical ingredients, and many others, how can we account for the fact that full-scale radical interpretations of World War II are so few in number?

A partial answer to this puzzling question may be afforded by the observation that, with the unexpected success of Hitler's counterrevolution in Germany (rather than a "genuine" revolution of the Left), it seemed more urgent for radicals to account for Fascism than for the war. We may understand this priority when we consider the stress placed by radical theory on connections between domestic affairs and foreign policy. How is it possible, a radical would ask, to understand the causes of an international conflict before coming to full knowledge of the domestic conditions of the warring nations?

In any case, radicals have invariably seen capitalism and Fascism in a close cause-effect relationship. Marxist-Leninists have tended to argue that, because of the imperatives of monopoly capitalism, a decadent middle class was forced to adopt Fascism as a response to the loss of colonial markets abroad and to the pressures of an increasingly militant proletariat at home.[72] Social Democrats have attempted to explain the appeal of Fascism, particularly to the lower middle class, by pointing to the psychological consequences of contemporary economic and political changes. Less concerned with the psychological dimension of social reality, but committed nonetheless to the moderate Marxism of the Social Democrats, was Franz Neumann (1900-1954), author of the now classic study of Nazism, *Behemoth* (1942). Heavily influenced by the left wing historian Eckart Kehr,

72. See, for example, Nicos Poulantzas, *Fascism and Dictatorship* (London: New Left Books, 1974), an analysis of fascism within the terms of the class struggle though not in an economically deterministic manner. Also see Jane Caplan, "Theories of Fascism: Nicos Poulantzas as Historian," *History Workshop: A Journal of Socialist Historians*, 3 (Spring 1977), pp. 83-100.

Neumann stressed the increased cartelization of German big business during the Weimar period. This process created an unstable economic situation that forced the Nazis to use the state to strengthen the monopolistic position of major industries in order to avert rebellion by the discontented masses. "The German economy of today," argued Neumann, "has two broad and striking characteristics. It is a monopolistic economy—*and* a command economy. It is a private capitalistic economy, regimented by the totalitarian state. We suggest as a name best to describe it, 'Totalitarian Monopoly Capitalism.'" Thus, for Neumann, Nazism was a continuation of monopoly capitalism, and the Nazi response to the real and potential class conflicts of Germany moved that nation toward war.[73]

Regardless of the varied explanations of this phenomenon advanced by radicals, however, their concentration on the nature of a particular social movement resulted in a lack of attention to international ramifications. Furthermore, in the Soviet Union, where Marxist-Leninist interpretations might have been forthcoming in the 1940s and 1950s, serious historical writing about World War II had to await Stalin's demise.

A number of recent developments indicate an increasing use of radical theory in the writing of World War II history. The first and most obvious of these is the publication in the

73. For works on fascism within the Social Democratic tradition that stress the importance of psychology, see Erich Fromm, *Escape From Freedom* (New York: Avon, 1941); and Theodor W. Adorno, *The Authoritarian Personality* (New York: Harper, 1950). For Social Democratic analysis that acknowledges the crucial role of economics in capitalist society (while rejecting economic determinism), see Franz Neumann's *Behemoth: The Structure and Practice of National Socialism* (London: V. Gollancz, 1942); the quotation is from p. 214. Also see discussions of *Behemoth* in Paul M. Sweezy, *The Present as History: Essays and Reviews on Capitalism and Socialism* (New York: Monthly Review Press, 1953), pp. 233-241, which initially appeared in *Science and Society*, 6 (Summer 1942); and Martin Jay, *The Dialectical Imagination: A History of the Frankfurt School and the Institute for Social Research, 1923-1950* (Boston: Little, Brown, 1973), Chap. 5 ("The Institute's Analysis of Nazism").

mid-1960s of the official Russian history of the conflict, *The History of the Great Patriotic War of the Soviet Union, 1941-1945*, a multi-volume study that is presently being revised.[74] Completely apart from this event, however, a new generation of radical Western scholars (and some liberal ones, as well) has now begun to produce monographs based on the view that foreign policy should be analyzed in its socioeconomic context, as a response to internal developments. A good example of this new approach, as it is applied to the diplomacy of the 1930s, is William Carr's *Arms, Autarky and Aggression: A Study in German Foreign Policy, 1933-1939* (1972). Though Carr believes it is too simple to view Hitler as merely "the helpless puppet of monopoly capitalism," he even more strongly rejects the conservative assumptions underlying the work of such great historians of Imperial Germany as Treitschke and Mommsen. Carr prefers to stress the primacy not of foreign policy but of internal policy:

To suppose that one man by sheer force of personality alone forced his views on the mass of the people would betray an equal lack of historical insight. The truth is that Hitler was the product of a particular socio-economic situation. Overwhelmed by an economic disaster which shook the capitalist system to its foundations, large numbers of Germans turned to Hitler as to a saviour.[75]

In a similar vein, after warning against attempts to explain foreign policy in purely economic terms, West German historian Klaus Hildebrand emphasizes in his recent work, *The Foreign Policy of the Third Reich* (1973), that "we cannot write a purely political history, abstracted from social and economic preconditions."[76]

This is certainly not to suggest that William Carr, Klaus

74. *Istoriia Voliko-Otechestvennoi Voiny Sovetskogo Souiza, 1941-1945*, 6 vols. (Moscow: Institute of Marxism-Leninism, 1963-1965). See also a current and expanded Soviet history of World War II by A. A. Grechko *et al., Istoriia vtoroi mirovoi voiny, 1939-1945* [*History of the Second World War*], 12 vols. (Moscow: Ministry of Defense, 1974-present).

75. William Carr, *Arms, Autarky and Aggression*, p. 6.

76. Klaus Hildebrand, *The Foreign Policy of the Third Reich*, p. 10.

Hildebrand, and some other younger historians are budding Marxist-Leninists. But it is to point out that radical (and left-liberal) assumptions about the origins of foreign policy and the causes of war are becoming important in historical writing about World War II.

The Orthodox Class Conflict Interpretation: the Soviet Version. The earliest Soviet interpretation of prewar diplomacy appeared in 1945 with the publication of a semi-official volume entitled *History of Diplomacy*. In this work the Western powers were accused of having tried to direct Hitler's aggressive intentions against the Soviet Union: "The compliancy of Anglo-French diplomacy encouraged Hitlerite Germany to further realization of its aggressive plans. Among the participants of the Munich Conference there was obvious understanding as to the direction of the German attack."[77] In this immediate postwar period, Soviet accounts not only minimized Allied participation in the war, but sought also to portray the Allies as crypto-enemies of the Soviet Union. The real aim of Western policy, according to these accounts, was to isolate the U.S.S.R. and to involve the Russians in war with Germany.

This Soviet position on the war mirrored the antagonisms of postwar politics. Indeed, diminished cooperation with the West meant that historical treatments of the war had to be postponed in favor of an intensive propaganda assault on the British and Americans. Joseph Stalin (1879-1953) established what written history there was. In a speech of February 1946, for example, Stalin declared: "It would be incorrect to think that the Second World War arose accidentally, or as the result of mistakes of one or another state figure. . . . As a matter of fact, the war arose as the inevitable result of the development of world economic and political forces on

77. See V. P. Potemkin *et al.* (eds.), *Istoriya diplomatii*, 3 vols. (Moscow, 1945), Vol. 3, p. 654, as cited in Matthew P. Gallagher, *The Soviet History of World War II* (New York: Frederick A. Praeger, 1963), p. 26.

the basis of contemporary monopolistic capitalism."[78] The Soviet leader was careful to distinguish between democratic and Fascist states, yet his analysis had the effect of lumping together all capitalist states in the same hostile category. For all practical purposes, Stalin's wartime writings and speeches collected in *The Great Patriotic War of the Soviet Union*, the last edition of which was published in 1949, were the only official history of the war during his lifetime.

Equally important for the Soviet view in the long run, however, was a booklet published by the government in 1948: *Falsificators of History*. Designed specifically to refute the United States Department of State's publication, *Nazi-Soviet Relations, 1939-1941*, this pamphlet and its supporting documents became a leading source for subsequent Russian historical writing. As in previous official statements, the prewar diplomacy of the Western powers was severely criticized. British, French, and especially American leaders were portrayed as seeking their own security at the expense of smaller states and as working to encourage Hitler's designs in eastern Europe. The Soviet Union thus had no recourse but to sign a nonaggression pact with Hitler aimed at erecting an "eastern front" against Nazi expansionism. According to Matthew Gallagher, author of a detailed study of Soviet historiography of World War II, *Falsificators of History* provided the concepts, the data, and even the phraseology for later Soviet interpretations of the war. "Henceforth," writes Gallagher, "the U.S. could not only share the blame with the other Allies, but would become the chief culprit in the Soviet historical indictment of the Allied role in the war."[79]

Gallagher also points out that from 1946 until near the end of Stalin's life in 1953, World War II "was virtually a forbidden topic for Soviet professional historians." And even when the topic began to be explored by scholars in the

78. See "Speech Delivered by J. V. Stalin at a Meeting of Voters," quoted in Gallagher, *The Soviet History of World War II*, p. 63.
79. Gallagher, *The Soviet History of World War II*, p. 63.

Soviet Union, he says, the requirements of the Communist Party's political criteria took precedence over unrestricted historical analysis, a situation that provoked considerable "organized resistance by the historical community to the Party's ideological campaign."[80]

With Stalin's death and the end of the "cult of personality," however, the new Soviet leadership tentatively began a reassessment of the origins and impact of World War II, in particular, and of Soviet military-strategic policies, in general. As a result, not only was Stalin's role in the war soon downplayed, but the contributions of the Allies were also increasingly acknowledged. Yet no softening of the traditionally hostile view of Western behavior accompanied these revisions. In fact, in some respects Soviet attitudes hardened, as is demonstrated by the May 1955 issue of *Questions in History*, containing the first formal public instructions regarding reevaluation of World War II: "Study and popularization of the history of the Great Patriotic War will help strengthen the Soviet people's military preparedness to crush any imperialist aggressor, and will help further to train the Soviet people in unshakable faith in the victory of their just cause and in ardent Soviet patriotism and proletarian internationalism."[81]

This new approach to the study of World War II received further impetus from the general break with Stalin, dramatized by Khrushchev's secret speech to the Twentieth Party Congress in 1956 denouncing the former Soviet leader. The anti-Stalinist campaign, however, also produced a conservative reaction within the Soviet Union among those who were deeply alarmed about its possible repercussions throughout the world. When the Hungarian revolt revealed the depth of the internal disagreement, the revisionist movement was quickly and sharply curtailed, even though its conclusions were not officially renounced.

80. *Ibid.*, p. 100.
81. See "O razrabotke istorii velikoy otechestvennoy voyny Sovetskogo soyuza," *Voprosy Istorii*, 5 (Moscow, 1955), p. 8, cited in Gallagher, *The Soviet History of World War II*, p. 138.

It was not until 1957 that the Soviet leadership felt sufficiently self-confident once again to encourage new interpretations of military and diplomatic history. In September
1957, in fact, the Central Committee announced its sponsor-
ship of a new multi-volume history of World War II, and the
creation of a special section in the Institute of Marxism-
Leninism to prepare it. This announcement in effect marked
the beginning of a new era in Soviet historical writing.

The initial question posed by Russian historians at this
time regarded the reasons for the Soviet Union's involvement in the war. Was the war simply one of defense against
the hostile imperialist forces of the West, as Stalin had
argued in his speech of 1946? This Stalinist interpretation
had already been confirmed by a major historical work of
the postwar period, *Essays on the History of the Great
Patriotic War* (1955), in which the Soviet Union's involvement was justified as resistance to the Fascists' alleged goals
of world domination and subjugation of other peoples.[82] Yet
this version came under searching review as preparations
began for the multi-volume history.

When the new Soviet history was finally published in the
mid-1960s, it offered an expanded, slightly modified, and
more sophisticated analysis of the pre-1941 period. The
coming of the war was now explained in terms of two basic
contradictions, the first being the expansionist pressure of
Germany, Italy, and Japan against the Versailles settlement
of the First World War, and the second, the rise of a
socialist Soviet Union in a still largely capitalist world.
According to this account, Germany, which had suffered a
serious defeat in World War I, as well as Italy and Japan,
which had been left out when the victors distributed the
spoils of war, demanded a new division of the world. However, the old colonial powers—Great Britain and France,
and the newest capitalist nation-state, the United States—
were in no way prepared to accept such a division. On the
contrary they attempted to expand their areas of control in

82. See Gallagher, *The Soviet History of World War II*, p. 165.

order to eliminate the competing imperialism of Germany, Italy, and Japan from the international arena. In this manner, a struggle for world domination flared up between these two groups of imperialist powers. Meanwhile, the Soviet Union's growing power constituted a new and significant factor that sharply distinguished the situation preceding World War II from that preceding World War I. In other words, along with the antagonisms that continued to divide the imperialists, there now existed a new source of difficulty: the fundamental antagonism between the two socioeconomic systems of capitalism and socialism. This situation led the "reactionary forces" of the West to unite in trying to use Germany as a weapon against Communist Russia. Hitler, however, refused to play the game according to Western expectations, launching instead a war against his imperialist competitors. The West, in turn, was stimulated by Hitler's attack on Poland to defend its imperialist position.

In this Marxist-Leninist explanation, then, the war's origins are traced to a clash between imperialist powers, a clash made inevitable (as Lenin had noted) by the natural laws of social development within the capitalist system. Furthermore, the Soviet Union is portrayed as preventing the formation of a united imperialist bloc by agreeing to the German-Soviet nonaggression pact in 1939. This "diplomatic victory" enabled the Russians simultaneously to weaken imperialism, strengthen socialism, and secure for themselves nearly two years of peace. By such a maneuver the Soviet Union was able to resolve these volatile international disputes, at least for a time.[83]

83. See the summary in *ibid.*, pp. 166-168, and the brief account of the nonaggression pact in J. P. Nettl, *The Soviet Achievement* (New York: Harcourt, Brace and World, 1967), pp. 155-156. We are indebted to Ms. Mikki Borton and Mr. Loren Okroi, graduate students in the Department of History at the University of California, Irvine, for translating extensive sections from the official Soviet history, cited in footnote 74 above. We have used here materials especially from pp. 16-22. A more popular version of this official history for use by Soviet secondary school students has

The Revisionist Class Conflict Interpretation: Lloyd Gardner, T. W. Mason, and Klaus Hildebrand. In Chapter 3, having called attention to the surprising lack of Social Democratic, "revisionist" theorizing about the causes of war, we drew upon George Lichtheim and others to construct what we believe to be a contemporary version of such a theoretical position. An informed Social Democrat would undoubtedly argue, we said, that to understand war one must first reject the mistaken notion that monopoly capitalism *inevitably* produces international conflict. Such a person would affirm, however, that the significance of capitalist institutions and of long-term structural factors must never be underestimated, for these will severely limit the options available to decision-makers. To determine the precise connections between domestic structures—particularly corporations and associated pressure groups—and international conflict is the historian's crucial assignment. Thus, while at times reaching conclusions similar to those of liberals strongly influenced by group conflict theory (such as John Kenneth Galbraith), a democratic socialist would be far more critical than they are of capitalism as an economic system.

As we have noted, just as Social Democratic *theory* about war is not plentiful, neither is Social Democratic *history* of World War II. Yet the outlines of such an interpretation, at least so far as Pearl Harbor is concerned, were sketched out as long ago as 1959 by William Appleman Williams in *The Tragedy of American Diplomacy* and were filled in to an extent in 1964 in *Economic Aspects of New Deal Diplomacy* by Lloyd Gardner (1923-   ), a former student of Williams at the University of Wisconsin, and now a Rutgers University historian.[84] In both these works the case is made for the war

recently been published in the Soviet Union and is the subject of Graham Lyons' *The Russian Version of the Second World War* (London: Archon, 1977).

84. William Appleman Williams, *The Tragedy of American Diplomacy*, 2nd ed. (New York: Dell, 1962), pp. 183-200. Gardner's book is cited in

having arisen from the clash of American and Japanese conceptions as to how the world should be organized economically. "The United States regarded the defense of its liberal trade system as central to the conduct of its foreign policy," Gardner suggests, whereas Japan was determined to have an Asian Empire because its leadership understandably had little faith in deriving substantial material benefits from "Open Door" arrangements.[85] To be sure, Gardner concedes, American political and corporate leaders did not want war with Japan, at least not before the "military matter in Europe is brought to a conclusion . . . ,"[86] but it was necessary to take a hard line with the Japanese in order to prevent them from driving the British from the Far East and, by controlling the "Chinese, Indian, and South Seas markets," weakening "our general diplomatic and strategic position."[87] In the end a creeping fatalism overcame both parties: "When President Roosevelt told the Japanese it was their turn to figure out ways and means of keeping the door open in Asia, the attack on Pearl Harbor was Tokyo's answer."[88] Gardner, then, presents a picture of the figures on both sides in which, while reacting to psychological as well as political factors, they are severely constrained by economic structures and beliefs. Though developments in the domestic situations are not used to explain the timing of war, the needs of the two nations' economies are absolutely central to the analysis.

Another historian to interpret the causes of World War II from a socioeconomic (though perhaps not avowedly Marxist) perspective is T. W. Mason (1940-   ), Fellow and Tutor

---

footnote 9 above. Note that Williams and Gardner are frequently identified by American historians as belonging to the "New Left." On this, see footnote 27 in Chapter 3, above.

85. Gardner, *Economic Aspects of New Deal Diplomacy*, p. 154.

86. *Ibid.*, p. 147. The quoted words are those of Undersecretary of State Sumner Welles.

87. *Ibid.*, p. 145. The quoted words are from a State Department memorandum of December 10, 1940.

88. *Ibid.*, p. 151.

in Modern History at Oxford since 1971, whose closely-reasoned critique of Taylor's *The Origins of the Second World War* appeared in 1964.[89] In this review Mason sternly chastized Taylor for resting his historical judgments almost solely upon diplomatic documents, and for ignoring Germany's economic preparations for war. Where Taylor had stressed Germany's military weakness in 1939, Mason asserted to the contrary that there could be "no doubt as to Germany's overwhelming military-economic preponderance in Europe in 1939."[90] In Mason's analysis, three structural changes in the German economy between 1929 and 1939 are crucial in understanding the causes of war: (1) the steadily growing predominance of the heavy industrial sector, (2) the trend toward autarchic self-sufficiency, and (3) the great increase in public spending. Thus, like other radical discussions of the origins of war, Mason's tends to focus on the domestic situation—on the economic, social, and political tensions *within* the Third Reich: "The only 'solution' open to the regime of the structural tensions and crises produced by dictatorship and rearmament was more dictatorship and more rearmament, then expansion, then war and terror, then plunder and enslavement."[91] "The sequence of international events was not thereby predetermined," cautions

89. See T. W. Mason, "Some Origins of the Second World War," *Past and Present*, 31 (December 1964), and reprinted in Esmonde M. Robertson (ed.), *The Origins of the Second World War*. Also see Mason, "Labor in the Third Reich, 1933-1939," *Past and Present*, 33 (April 1966), pp. 112-141; Mason, "National Socialism and the Working Class," *New German Critique*, 11 (Spring 1977), pp. 49-93; and Molly Nolan, "Class Struggles in the Third Reich," *Radical History Review*, 4 (Spring and Summer, 1977), pp. 138-159.

90. Mason, "Some Origins of the Second World War," p. 119. On this question see Burton H. Klein, *Germany's Economic Preparations for War* (Cambridge, Mass.: Harvard University Press, 1959); Arthur Schweitzer, *Big Business in the Third Reich* (Bloomington: Indiana University Press, 1964); Alan S. Milward, *The German Economy at War* (London: Athlone Press, 1965); and Berenice A. Carroll, *Design for Total War: Arms and Economics in the Third Reich* (The Hague: Mouton, 1968).

91. Mason, "Some Origins of the Second World War," p. 124.

Mason, "but the range of possibilities was severely circum-scribed."[92]

An analysis that stands slightly to the left of Mason's—though still well within the bounds of Social Democratic thought—is provided by the West German scholar Klaus Hildebrand (1941-   ). Hildebrand, Professor of Medieval and Modern History at the University of Frankfurt since 1974, is the author of three books, *From Commonwealth to Empire: Hitler, NSDAP and the Colonial Question, 1919-1945* (1969), *Bethmann-Hollweg* (1970), and, most recently, *The Foreign Policy of the Third Reich* (1973).

The Nazis' goals in the 1930s, Hildebrand contends, were "a product of those significant domestic and socio-political conditions inherent in the German Reich which had helped to determine German foreign policy ever since Bismarck." Taking a long-range historical perspective, Hildebrand argues that social conflicts in Germany were never genuinely resolved but instead were camouflaged "with the help of secondary integrating factors and mechanisms" that served to prevent meaningful social reforms from below.[93] In the years preceding World War I, nationalism had been sufficient to mobilize "the (petit-) bougeois class—in their dependent relation as employees—behind the Crown and the landowners and heavy industrialists who stood in alliance behind it." Thereafter, however, so thoroughly transformed was Germany by World War I, inflation, and world economic crisis in the 1930s, that "new tools of integration were necessary to tie down and commit 'the people' to the expansionist policy of its political rulers and the preservation of the social status quo connected to this policy." This became the socially-motivated function of the Hitler dictatorship.[94]

Hildebrand, while never removing Hitler to the historical sidelines, centers his attention not on the Führer's "demonic power," but instead on complex historical relations and

92. *Ibid.*, p. 125.
93. Hildebrand, *The Foreign Policy of the Third Reich*, p. 124.
94. *Ibid.*, p. 77.

conditions. His basic queries are two: Who determined the principles of foreign policy before and after 1933? And which interests decisively influenced decisions on foreign policy before and after January 30, 1933? In attempting to answer these closely related questions, Hildebrand does not portray a united German capitalist ruling class, as a Marxist-Leninist might have done, but writes instead of an "economic community" which included several groups with different interests.[95] He points out that ever since the Great Depression of 1893-1896 most leaders in Western industrial nations, including the United States, were well aware that territorial expansion and military production were valuable and proven methods of combating economic crises. In Germany it was also understood that overseas expansion and continental power would only be possible after the creation of a strong army. "Since socio-economic necessities thus played such an integral role in [Hitler's world-view]," continues Hildebrand, he "ultimately regarded rearmament as the most important precondition for his expansionist Programme."[96] Hitler's policies therefore satisfied Germany's desires for national recovery, but they also "suited the economic interests of a bourgeois society dependent on permanent industrial growth."[97]

To the drives for expansion and military production Hildebrand adds a third motivating force behind the foreign policy of the Third Reich—ideology based on racist dogma: "Of all the types of integrating mechanisms applied in the history of Prussia-Germany, anti-semitism . . . was the most powerful."[98] In his view, this anti-semitic racial ideology, while extremely important in its own right, also served to deflect attention from defects in the existing social order. In a recent review (1976) of Norman Rich's two-volume work, *Hitler's War Aims*, Hildebrand has reiterated this position while rejecting (with surprising vigor) Marxist-Leninist approaches:

95. *Ibid.*, p. 10.   96. *Ibid.*, p. 27.
97. *Ibid.*, pp. 44, 65.   98. *Ibid.*, p. 124.

Far from being the key to all understanding, the attempt to apply the orthodox Marxist formula of state monopoly capitalism or to use Hilferding's theorem of "organized capitalism" not only when dealing with the age of so-called classical imperialism but also increasingly with respect to the history of the Third Reich and the international events of the 1930s and 1940s, thereby attributing the origins and growth of National Socialism primarily to economic factors, would appear, in the light of Rich's very plausible arguments in favor of the absolute primacy of politics, to be more of an obstacle than a help. For Hitler's intention and the task of National Socialism was not to uphold a particular economic or social structure, which—however openly admitted—is inherent in every Marxist-oriented interpretation. Rather, notwithstanding considerations of economic expediency, it was to realize racial supremacy on a global scale. . . . Rich demonstrates with unusual clarity that in the final analysis it was the idea of race which dominated Hitler's policy and conduct of war.[99]

It is therefore within a triangle formed by economics, politics, and ideology that Hildebrand seeks to analyze the foreign policy of the Third Reich and the origins of World War II. All three factors are involved in his definitions of the classes and groups that were of prime importance in guiding Germany. There thus are obviously elements of liberal group conflict theory to be found in Hildebrand's historical interpretation. But there is an even more evident emphasis—characteristic of radical scholarship—upon long-range socioeconomic tensions and the domestic functions of international conflict. Hitler's program is described as representative of all the political demands emerging in Germany since 1866-1871: demands for an economic empire in Europe; for Central Africa as an area of expansion; for a policy of rearmament as a means of stimulating the economy; for the use of foreign policy in reinforcing the socioeconomic status quo. "Looking back," Hildebrand concludes:

Hitler's Programme was only apparently independent of motivations with German society; in fact it emerges as an expression of the sum of demands and wishes of that society, ordered into a

99. See Hildebrand, "Hitler's War Aims," *The Journal of Modern History*, 46 (September 1976), pp. 522-530.

political and military strategy by the Dictator. Thus the continental and overseas demands of Hitler's Programme place it completely within a particular tradition of power politics such as is
observable in Prussian-German history since the days of
Bismarck.[100]

The author's implication seems to be *not* that Germany was
insufficiently liberal and therefore a threat to its neighbors,
but rather that Germany was *both* pre-liberal *and* liberal,
and therefore even more dangerous than if it had been
either.

CONCLUDING REMARKS

Evaluating, as we have, these several histories of the two
world wars from the standpoint of our ideological and
theoretical categories puts the interpretations in a new and
different light. We are able to observe that the traditional
concerns of historians, not to speak of the emotional battles
over such matters as war-guilt, have often obscured the
kinds of issues historians ought to be considering. We can
discern that historians who have been thought to be totally
at odds in their viewpoints have sometimes in fact had a
surprising amount in common. Clearly, then, much of the
historiographical struggle has been carried on within a
remarkably narrow ideological and theoretical range. Furthermore, lack of explicit interest in ideology and theory on
the part of historians has robbed them of incentive to test
alternative explanations, to hypothesize about the causes
that lay behind the causes, to ask the same questions of
different authors and structures, and to render explicit the
linkages between and among the various enumerated factors. Ideology clearly conditions the writing of history, both
through historians' "common sense" and through the formal
theory they imbibe. But until historians are able to become
more conscious of their ideological and theoretical inclinations they are likely to be more the victims than the bene-
ficiaries of the process.

100. Hildebrand, *The Foreign Policy of the Third Reich*, p. 81.

Epilogue

There remain a number of things to do. We want to empha-size once again, by means of argument and example, that the approach we have been using can be effectively em-ployed in studying the causal histories of all wars. We also wish to stress its applicability to scholarship concerned with other social phenomena, such as the *impact* of war or the outbreak of revolution. Finally, we would like to offer a few thoughts of our own regarding the origin and process of war. We do this realizing full well that to "practice what we preach" we must candidly examine our own ideologies, even becoming autobiographical in order to illuminate our as-sumptions and perspectives.

It would be false to claim that we had tested our analytic approach on the historiographies of countless wars. Never-theless, we *have* utilized it in other cases than those dis-cussed above, and with success enough to make us confident that further application will only confirm its usefulness.

In particular we have been pleased with what our cate-gories have enabled us to learn about historical writing on the Vietnam War. They have allowed us to discern, for example, that not all the "hawks" of the 1960s were con-servatives (witness W. W. Rostow) and that not all the "doves" were on the left (note Hans Morgenthau).[1] They have helped us to recognize how many "liberal" values Arthur Schlesinger, Jr., and Daniel Ellsberg have in com-mon, despite the severity of their debate over the "Quagmire

1. See Walt W. Rostow, *View from the Seventh Floor* (New York: Harper and Row, 1964); Rostow, *The Diffusion of Power: An Essay in Recent History* (New York: Macmillan, 1972); Hans Morgenthau, *A New Foreign Policy for the United States* (New York: Frederick A. Praeger, 1969); and Morgenthau, *Truth and Power: Essays of a Decade, 1960-1970* (New York: Frederick A. Praeger, 1970).

Myth and the Stalemate Machine."[2] They have forced us to
realize to what extent a book like David Halberstam's *The
Best and Brightest*, despite its engaging qualities, reflects the
fact that its assumptions and theory are implicit and confused.[3] They have permitted us to admire the efforts of
Robert Galluci in *Neither Peace Nor Honor* to conduct a
theoretically precise study while disagreeing with the author
(for *ideological* reasons) about which factors are most important.[4] In short, both of us and our students have profited
greatly from having used ideological and sub-ideological
categories in our analysis of historians' work regarding the
causes of the war.

There seems no reason, moreover, why this same approach would not be equally valid and revealing in studying
the theory and history of such recurrent phenomena as
restorations, reform movements, crime waves, and the like.
If one were to examine what has been done in analyzing the
impact of war, for instance, one should be able to develop a
set (or sets) of theoretical parameters for the subject, worked
out from and based upon explicit ideological foundations.
Thus, one would probably find that conservative theorists
assess the impact of war almost entirely in terms of how it
has affected the distribution of power (both domestically
and internationally), the strength of the leading classes and
nations, and the sense of hierarchy and proper subordination among other parties. One would surely discover that
liberal theorists devote their attention to how the conflict
has helped to establish or disestablish liberal regimes, increase or reduce frustrations, misperception, or social (inter-

2. See Arthur Schlesinger, Jr., "Eyeless in Indochina," *New York
Review of Books* (October 21, 1971); Schlesinger, *The Bitter Heritage* (New
York: Fawcett, 1968); and Daniel Ellsberg, *Papers on the War* (New York:
Pocket Books, 1972), pp. 41-141.

3. David Halberstam, *The Best and the Brightest* (New York: Random
House, 1972).

4. Robert L. Galluci, *Neither Peace Nor Honor: The Politics of
American Military Policy in Vietnam* (Baltimore: Johns Hopkins University Press, 1975).

national) integration, and produce a balanced or unbalanced international system. One would undoubtedly determine that radical theorists focus on how the war has advanced or set back the course of revolution, strengthened the working class or the capitalist class, and destroyed or created economic resources. In point of fact, of course, the field of impact of war studies is so relatively new that there is not a greal deal of theory *per se* in existence. Or, to put it another way, rather than being able to rely on creative ideologists or social scientists (as in the case of war causation), historians in this realm are often in the position of having to invent their own theory as they write their history. What this means, among other things, is that as observers we are not as richly provided with either theoretical or historical examples for our categories as we were in working with the causes of war. It may also mean, however, that the availability of our approach will be more important to practitioners in the new field than to those in the old.

To be sure, we do not wish to imply that there are not many ingenious and impressive theoretical statements with regard to the effects of war. One could hardly survey the offerings of such authors as Peter Loewenberg,[5] Lewis Coser,[6] Stanislav Andreski,[7] Arthur Marwick,[8] and Jürgen Kocka[9] (not to mention Tocqueville, Lenin, and other clas-

5. Peter Loewenberg, "The Psychohistorical Origins of the Nazi Youth Cohort," *American Historical Review*, 75 (December 1971), pp. 1457-1502. See also Arno J. Mayer, "Internal Causes and Purposes of War in Europe, 1870-1956: A Research Assignment," *Journal of Modern History*, 41 (September 1969), pp. 291-303; and Peter Loewenberg, "Arno J. Mayer's Internal Causes and Purposes of War in Europe, 1870-1956—An Inadequate Model of Human Behavior, National Conflict, and Historical Change," *Journal of Modern History*, 42 (December 1970), pp. 628-636.

6. Lewis Coser, *The Functions of Social Conflict* (Glencoe, Ill.: Free Press, 1956). See also Coser, *Continuities in the Study of Social Conflict* (New York: Free Press, 1967).

7. Stanislaw Andrzejewski (later changed to Stanislav Andreski), *Military Organization and Society* (London: Routledge and Paul, 1954).

8. See Arthur Marwick, *War and Social Change in the Twentieth Century: A Comparative Study of Britain, France, Germany, Russia, and the United States* (London: Macmillan, 1974).

9. Jürgen Kocka, *Klassengesellschaft im Krieg: Deutsche Sozialgeschichte 1914-1918* (Göttingen: Vandenhoeck und Ruprecht, 1973).

sic figures)[10] without acknowledging that much has been accomplished. Still, many of the propositions put forward are partial in nature, with unanalyzed assumptions and undiagnosed implications. There is ample opportunity here for future theory builders and theory testers.

Having made a case for the relevance of our categorizations to that distinct phenomenon called impact of war, let us confess that we ourselves would much prefer to think of war's causes and effects together. To make satisfactory comparisons from war to war we believe that it is necessary to perceive war as a unified and total phenomenon and to avoid when possible compartmentalizing it into its coming and its going. Just as a doctor thinks of a disease as a unity, from its incubation through the patient's convalescence, we consider war an experience with real continuity of character from the earliest to the final stages of development.

But this brings us to a point at which, in order to proceed, we must become somewhat more personal. To cast an adequate light on our theory we must discuss our ideology, and specifically we must acknowledge that we locate ourselves ideologically slightly to the left of that fuzzy line which separates the "left" liberal from the revisionist radical. We recognize that we are to a degree ambivalent about the world of scholarship and the society in which we live. We feel simultaneously appreciative and critical, patient and impatient, somewhat relativistic yet in the end committed to putting together an understanding of society that can serve as a platform for an activist and reform-oriented life. Our attitudes are undoubtedly in large measure a function of our nationality, generation, and class, for we are both Americans born in the 1930s, reared in conservative (i.e., right-liberal) middle income homes, educated in public schools and private universities, and exposed to the radicalizing experience of the anti-Vietnam War movement at a time when we were not too old to be deeply affected by it. Mean-

10. See Leon Bramson and George W. Goethals (eds.), *War: Studies from Psychology, Sociology, and Anthropology* (New York: Basic Books, 1964).

while, we are eclectic enough that one of us retains a church affiliation and both of us strongly endorse the traditionalists' affirmation of community (which we see as a value they hold in common with the radicals).

Writing this book has reinforced our inclination toward eclecticism, for it has left us with enhanced respect for each of the three great ideological traditions and for the theorists and historians who labor within them. Perhaps our synthetic urge was also earlier strengthened by the way in which liberal graduate schools train their historians to be multifactoral in interpretation, that is, to explain events by citing a multiplicity of causes, each of which is said to be "partly responsible." At any rate, though we find ourselves particularly impressed by revisionist socialists' values and their arguments regarding war (especially by the socialist emphasis on the ability of the privileged elites to design national policies for their own protection), we are also possessed of an admiration for certain conservative and liberal insights and a desire to integrate these into our "soft radical" perspective. Olin is slightly more interested in economic relationships, Nelson in psychological, but the motivation is similar in both of us. We want to be genuinely synthetic, not syncretic. We flatter ourselves that an increasing awareness of the role of ideology and theory in writing history will enable us (and others), not to escape these factors, but to develop more comprehensive and effective versions of each. The more sophisticated the ideology, the better can be the theory.

So, with this preface, and to point up the fact that our analysis is intended to encourage theoretical speculation (as it has encouraged us to speculate), let us sketch our own picture of the historical process with particular attention to the role of war. Such a scheme would postulate, among other things, that contemporary societies are characterized by long-term cycles in public moods, alternations related loosely to certain specific kinds of events. Such moods, or emotional sets, are partly conscious and partly unconscious and are never uniformly present but are shared by various groups and classes to the extent that they share backgrounds and experiences.

This thesis suggests that over a period of time societies tend to move through the following phases: (1) a period of relative satisfaction/confidence, in which the majority feel themselves capable of coping with the change occuring within and about them; (2) a period of disappointment/ anxiety, in which (perhaps because of a depression, notice-able concentration of wealth, etc.) large numbers lose their sense of comprehending and/or being in a good relationship to societal change; (3) a period of dissatisfaction/aggression I, in which movements are organized for purposes of domes-tic reform while others mobilize in defense of the status quo; (4) a period of dissatisfaction/aggression II, in which do-mestic reform may be shunted aside and the nation united in attempting to improve its external environment through war or aggressive foreign policy; (5) a period of exhaustion/ anxiety (unless the war or equivalent activity is very brief and successful), in which the populace, weary and disori-ented by growing confusion, despairs of large group efforts; and (6) a period of relaxation/adjustment, in which the majority accommodate or reconcile themselves to the changed situation which has resulted and which no one foresaw or desired. This phase in turn gradually transforms itself into a new period of relative satisfaction.[11]

This hypothesis should not obscure the fact that elites are at all times involved in trying to manipulate other elements of the population, or the public mood itself, so as to perpetuate themselves in power or to bolster existing institutions. Indeed, in countries where traditional (or even nontraditional) elites remain established, reform move-ments often seem to accomplish little more than to increase

11. With regard to the two wars which we have studied, the phasing might be worked out roughly as follows for western Europe: (1) 1876-1890, 1924-1929; (2) 1890-1900, 1929-1933; (3) 1900-1910, 1933-1938; (4) 1910-1916, 1938-1944; (5) 1916-1924, 1944-1948; (6) 1924-1929, 1948-1956.

the probability that elites will finally follow their own "ultras" and embark upon an effort to unite the nation against a foreign enemy. In the more liberal, Western nations, reform movements more frequently wend their way to power only to discover that their inability to solve the basic problems of capitalist society (e.g., increasing inequality, alienation) renders them vulnerable to being outflanked by conservatives who urge the use of force abroad and who therefore tempt them to espouse it themselves.

In both instances the results can be predicted. A declaration of war creates an almost irresistible tendency for the citizenry to rally behind the country's leadership, and, if the war is a triumph and quickly over, the victory will greatly buttress the prestige of the leaders. Only when a war continues into a second or third year will serious weariness and opposition begin to appear, usually voiced by the political Left and often of such proportions as seriously to impair the war effort. Even so, unless the opponents of the war are able to seize power and maintain themselves by force (as in Russia in 1917), the growth of pacifism will ultimately engender a reaction in the name of patriotism and discipline, especially vigorous among those groups (like the middle classes) which identify strongly with the nation. Such a "counterreaction" will frequently carry a nation through to victory or at least to an image-preserving settlement of the war. In the event of a national defeat the counterreaction may lose its controlling position and temporarily go underground, but it will reappear in later months. In more typical situations the counterreaction will gradually relax its grip, at the same time helping to establish the tone and techniques of the early postwar era.

Here, then, is a sketchy model with elements of theory that we may have seen more often in other contexts. It presents historical change, at least in the Western world, in terms of a largely uni-directional capitalist thrust, but in any case as a process supporting alternating national moods (epiphenomena tied to economic occurrences as well as major social experiences), with both thrust and moods playing a role in bringing on domestic and international violence. It may sound almost conservative with its implication that rapid change is disorienting. Moreover, it obviously incorporates a social-psychological perspective with its emphasis on anxiety, misunderstanding, and displacement of emotions. Yet it also suggests that capitalism has more problems than other economic orders and that there is a very conscious and frequently successful endeavor on the part of possessing classes to guide/direct the feelings and demands of others for their own purposes. Though events in international relations are not considered central factors, they can clearly be important to the extent that one nation's necessities impinge on those of another.

The crucial questions for the reader, of course, are these: Does such an ambitious vision violate your own ideological predilections? Does it flow logically from its own ideological foundations? Is it, or can it be, internally consistent? Can it be tested, and if and when it is, does it accord with historical reality?

Index